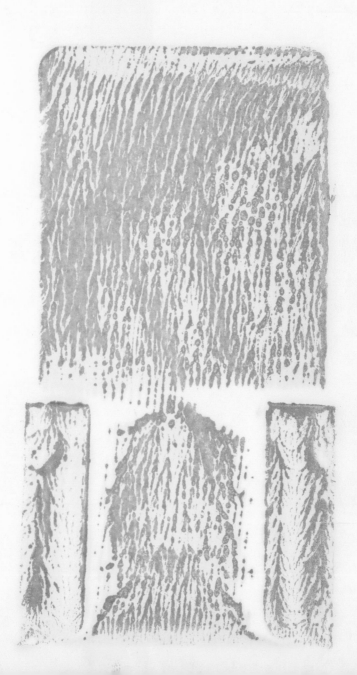

More Fun for Older Adults

Association Press / New York

MORE FUN
for
OLDER ADULTS

By
Virginia Stafford
and
Larry Eisenberg

Illustrations by BLANCHE SLOAN

More Fun for Older Adults

Publisher's stock number: 1616

Library of Congress catalog card number: 66-20473

Printed in the United States of America

Dedicated

with appreciation and affection

to

THE REV. AND MRS. M. LEO RIPPY

whose vision of the possibilities
for joyful older adult activity
and whose labor for this cause
have brightened the lives of thousands of folks
across the nation

and to

THE LATE MRS. CARRIE S. STAFFORD

whose love of fun enriched so many lives
in the classroom, the church, and the community
and, not the least, in her home and family.

Foreword

. . . . This is a book of ideas and activities designed to put an extra measure of zest into the lives of older folks, both in groups and at home.

We have attempted both to answer numerous requests for ideas and activities and to carry over many of the games that were submitted to us by older adults themselves. Some of these contributors are not now living, but we are sure that they would be glad that their joy lives on.

Especially do we appreciate the lively drawings of Blanche Sloan, updated from our earlier *Fun for Older Adults*. Some of the activities and ideas in this book are borrowed from that work as well.

We should like to express special appreciation to Virginia Musselman of the National Recreation and Park Association for her very practical suggestions to our outline; to Virginia Gregory of the North Carolina Recreation Commission in Raleigh for sharing a variety of materials; to Mrs. Lillie M. Taylor of the Washington State Council on Aging for things she sent us, particularly Margaret White's excellent bulletin; to Dr. Harry Edgren, long-time friend at Purdue; to Mrs. Thelma Hall, and to Helen and Laren Eisenberg for secretarial assistance.

We express gratitude to these contributors also: George Adams, Mrs. F. O. Byfield, Mrs. T. P. Battle, Dr. Ira Barnett, Mrs. Foster

7

Brown, Mrs. Ruth Bible, Mrs. J. B. Cleaver, Dr. Cecil Leslie Clifford, Mrs. Lela Connolly, Mrs. C. V. Cochran, Mrs. A. L. Beckendorf, Dr. Harold A. Ehrensperger, R. B. DeLaney, Mrs. T. L. Folks, Mrs. C. L. Fuhrman, Mrs. C. L. Gardner, Miss Ella Gardner, Mrs. Edna Giese, Miss Jane Farwell.

Albert Heuvel, Mrs. W. F. Huiet, Mrs. R. E. Harllee, Robert Hean, Mrs. John Hacker, Harris A. Jones, Mrs. Carl Keen, Mrs. Eva Koepp, Mr. and Mrs. J. A. Joyner, Ronald Johnson, Oscar Lungren, Mr. and Mrs. B. T. Kumler, Bert Lyle, Mrs. Pauline Lackey, Lillie Martin, Mr. and Mrs. F. B. Kruse, Bertie Miller, Mrs. E. W. McElmurray, Sr., Mrs. Jennie Belle McRae, Mrs. Ray Murphy, Miss Fannie MacMunn, Mrs. Agnes Pylant, Mrs. Irene Reedy, Mrs. Lock C. Riehl, Mrs. Ardis Stevens, Mrs. C. B. Stewart, Mrs. B. N. Stitt, Roma G. Stafford, Mrs. J. F. Sargent, Mrs. Catherine Searles, Lynn Rohrbough, George J. Steinman, Mrs. Lillie Stoner, Florence A. Smith, Mrs. Jennie M. Tiesinger, Lillian M. Winn, John E. Wilson, Beryl W. Williams, and Mrs. S. A. Shackelford. We hope we have not missed any names.

We have been delighted to see the tremendous progress made in meeting the needs of older people in our population, with the success of the magazines *Modern Maturity, Harvest Years, Aging,* and *Mature Years* (see the listing of sources at the end of the book) and the increased interest of government and private agencies in helping to make the latter years of life rich and enjoyable.

VIRGINIA STAFFORD
LARRY EISENBERG

Nashville, Tennessee

Contents

The homebound can play too! . . . Games . . . Handwork . . . Reading aloud . . . Parties . . . Home fun for older people who aren't shut-ins

Organizations . . . Magazines and bulletins . . . Basic books for older people . . . Books in social recreation . . . Crafts . . . Equipment for fun . . . Films and plays . . . Music . . . General suggestions

Planning
the Fun

THE ORGANIZED OLDER ADULT FELLOWSHIP

. . . . One of the phenomena of recreation planning today is the establishment of numerous groups of older adults, call them clubs or what you will. The first ones were apparently started by men and women to provide companionship and offer status and recognition to individual older people.

Through the years the movement has grown to the point that a community without its Golden Age Club or "VIP's" is hard to find. For the most part these groups are stimulating and creative, a worthy part of the community's total recreation plan for its people.

Such groups, while they may be related to or offspring of a community center or other program for older folks, are not the entire agency's program, for in most cases the club group has stated meeting times, a name,* and somewhat patterned procedures.

FLEXIBLE STRUCTURE—THE FRAMEWORK FOR A HAPPY LIFE

Government subsidies and medical allowances cannot take the place of companionship, laughter, the fun of doing something useful and creative. No matter what our financial circumstances, we need lots of the spice that makes life really worth living. And that means companionship, fun, sharing.

The United States is moving toward a culture of leisure for all its people, young and old. For the employed person there will be increasing amounts of time at the end of the working day, on weekends, and in lengthy vacations. For the retired person whose time is mostly his own, the problem is one of planning his activities, definitely setting up his own routine of work, play, study, enrichment, individual interests, and group participation.

Most of us don't know how to play, what to do with unscheduled time. We haven't learned because we haven't had the freedom to do as we pleased—not till retirement came and suddenly we found the boss, the office, the school, the job refusing to set up our daily affairs for us anymore.

Here's where the club or organization for older adults comes in. Yours may be a community center, a church or temple fellowship group, a gardening or patriotic society. Almost any organization largely made up of retirees can help older people find what they're seeking, get into interesting activities, and be part of a stimulating program that makes the days exciting and eliminates the boredom of enforced unemployment.

---

* Some now in use: Young at Heart; JOY Fellowship (Just Older Youth); Evergreens; Elderberries; DMA's (Don't Mention Age); Friendship Circle; XYZ (Extra Years of Zest); Post Grads; Elderblooms; Live Wires; Jolly Seniors; Jolly Elders; The Diamond Set; Hilltoppers; Friendship Club; Gaytimers.

CONSIDER NEEDS

Older men and women, just like everyone else, have needs that recreation planning should keep in view. As we list these needs, we could be describing children or youth or young adults **except in degree of need,** for older people have a cluster of experiences that put this whole matter in slightly different focus.

Older people's needs are affected by changes in their family life due to loss of spouse and to mobility of children; changes in living quarters; retirement; lowered income (in most cases); physical changes; lessening social contacts; loss of daily routine formerly planned by others.

Every person needs to be loved; to show love; to have companionship; to make friends; to have a sense of self-respect and of being valued by others; to be independent; to be useful, needed; to feel wanted; to contribute to others' welfare; to achieve financial security; to laugh and play.

The older person, because of the changes that seem to zero in on his life all at once, experiences these needs to an acute degree. Procedures to meet these needs require insight, skill, and a deep interest in older people. The leader and the group develop these abilities as they interact, carry planned programs to completion, and candidly evaluate success.

PLANNING

Older adults must have a part in working out all recreation plans, from setting up the first committee to actually carrying out the chosen activity. The selection of planning committee members should be made by the older adults themselves. If the group desires, it may select some younger persons or other adults outside the organization to help with ideas and with setting up specific plans. A member of the agency's or organization's staff may be an adviser to the committee.

Tasks of the planning committee include these: evaluating the present program; surveying the interests of the members; assessing the resources available—in the group itself and in the community; outlining a program of activities; planning a specific event, including time, date, location, leadership, activities, equipment, refreshments; establishing subcommittees to handle various phases of the activity; publicizing the event; evaluating success after the event and pointing directions for future planning.

Careful planning helps achieve some important values such as these: comprehensiveness; balance; variety; newness, freshness; full participation; relationships across age lines so that old and young may enjoy each other; alternation of activity; inclusion of the ideas of the entire group, not just of one clique or point of view.

A good planning committee is therefore concerned over such uncreative practices as these: the same foursome playing cards or other games together and refusing to include a new person or to part with a particular table or location; certain individuals always withdrawing to the role of spectator, never being willing to participate; too much sitting at the TV, passively watching, often without real recognition of the programs' meaning or purpose.

LEADERSHIP

What of the leader of older adult recreation? Most clubs, community centers, and other agencies involving older adults have a staff person designated to assist this group. He has an essential role as adviser in planning and as assistant in carrying out activities. Whether he be young or near the older group's age, he should be a person capable of evaluating his own abilities, assessing the needs of the group, and establishing rapport with each individual. Let us look at some qualities such a recreation leader should have:

1. He is natural, entirely himself. He treats older people with natural friendliness.
2. He respects each person. He never condescends in tone,

word, or manner (no trite business about "You young boys and girls," for example!).

3. He seems to be having as good a time as anybody. There is no evidence that he could be better occupied elsewhere, or that he is sacrificing his time.

4. He takes physical disabilities into account but avoids unnecessary coddling or sympathizing. Wherever possible, he helps people to rely on themselves.

5. He speaks clearly, repeats instructions when needed, and patiently takes time to experiment with a game till all understand what to do.

6. He feels responsible for bringing new ideas and suggestions to the group. He realizes that many older adults have had limited leisure and play activity in the past, and need help to find interesting things to do.

7. He never forces a person to participate. He knows that many people share in the activity by watching others. He is alert, however, for a spark of interest and for evidence of desire to get into the game.

8. He never rushes the group from one thing to another, but gives folks time to enjoy each activity to the fullest. He is more concerned about enjoyment than about using all the games he has prepared.

9. He watches for peak moments in an activity and shifts to something new before people get bored.

10. He carefully avoids being always in the limelight. As quickly as possible, he turns over the leadership of an activity to a member of the group.

11. He is quick to praise, and watches for opportunities to acknowledge a good piece of work or a particular improvement.

12. He watches for the timid, is constantly on the lookout for something they can do to achieve status and to succeed in the group.

13. He tries never to do anything for the group that they can do for themselves.

14. He tries never to judge people hastily, but to seek out the cause of aggressiveness or other objectionable characteristics.

15. He avoids talking disparagingly about one person to another. He makes it his goal to help members of the group to become less critical of each other and more appreciative of everyone's contribution. In so doing, he encourages mutual frankness and acceptance.

MEETING ROOM AND EQUIPMENT

If possible, a room should be set aside for the group's exclusive use. If this is not possible, perhaps they can have a special closet for storing group treasures. They need it as well as the Scouts, for example, who often have this kind of privilege.

The planning committee may see that the group's meeting room has these features: street level, close to parking area; large, adaptable for small or large groups to be formed interchangeably; bright colors, tastefully decorated but not gaudy or lavish; well-lighted and -ventilated; wall-to-wall carpeting or smooth, not slick, floors; hot plate or kitchenette; rest room facilities near meeting room.

Equipment should include at least some of the following: sturdy folding tables (easily moved about and easily stored; some tables with adjustable height are desirable for wheel chair people); lightweight, but sturdy, movable chairs (straight chairs with arms, if possible; avoid deep-cushioned furniture that presents difficulty to the older person in sitting down and getting up); storage space (shelves for games, songbooks, etc.); songbooks (large print, if possible); movie and slide projectors; record players (including slow speed from associations for the blind); games (table game equipment, outdoor games); chalkboard, piano (autoharp, small organ); looms, ceramic kilns, quilting frames; permanent name tags to be used each time the group gathers; question box; case for displaying things made by members.

It is desirable that the group have its own library of reading material, if possible. A set of bookshelves mounted on casters could be rolled into a storage place when not in use.

Some groups make a lot of their bulletin boards, calling them "Inspiration Centers" and posting pictures, poems, religious materials, uplifting thoughts, and members' birthdays. Some also have books of clippings.

THESE THINGS ARE EASY TO FIND FOR HOME OR GROUP FUN

A little search around any home, church, or club will produce many things usable for bringing fun to older adults. Many of these objects can be had at the expense of nothing except effort. Browse through this list and check the ones which you could use—then use them! Many suggestions throughout this book require items like these:

1. Miscellaneous craft materials—scissors, paste, paints, aluminum foil, tubes from foil or gift wrappings, beads, ribbons, shells, dried seeds, dried grasses, spools, Christmas cards, paper plates, lollipop sticks, needles, thread, feathers, scraps of cloth, yarn, and leather, pipe cleaners, toothpicks, file cards, yard sticks, rug scraps.

2. Used magazines and catalogs. A group may work up a story from the advertisements, mount pictures by category for children's use, or make posters.

3. Record player and tape recorder. Fun for listening to all sorts of things—your own voice, old Caruso and Galli-Curci records, the latest hits.

4. Pen, ink, and stationery. Have them ready for members of the group to write to shut-ins, absentees, old friends, newcomers, other clubs of older adults.

5. Old newspapers. For patterns, funny costumes, papier-mâché objects, all sorts of uses.

6. Candles. Everybody has boxes of old candles. Remelted, they can be used to make all shapes and sizes of new candles.

Use old cups to make balls (two halves, then seal together with twine between for wick), milk cartons for large square ones, etc. Try the new art of dropping medium-sized crushed ice into the wax to make lacy-looking candles.

7. Old costumes. What once were "clothes" in time become "costumes." A box for everybody to deposit old hats, dresses, shoes, suits, etc., will be a constant source of fun for skits and plays.

8. Whittling materials—knives, wood, Ivory soap.

9. Game sets—checkers, Scrabble, jigsaw puzzles, anagrams, Parcheesi, Monopoly, dominoes, Flinch, Rook, etc.

10. Birthday candles and napkins. For celebrations in the group; or some folks may take a birthday cake and refreshments to a shut-in.

11. Old songbooks—the barbershop quartet kind, or some for "community sings."

12. Crepe paper, tissue paper, gilt stars, other leftovers still useful for decorations.

13. Tools, power and otherwise—chiefly for the men but available to anyone who feels creative.

14. Card tables. Easy to set up, easy to store.

15. Sturdy chairs, preferably with arms. Avoid folding chairs if you can, as they are difficult to sit in and aren't sure to "stay put" when a person tries to get up.

16. Watertight buckets and pans.

17. Muffin tins—useful for targets (each hole numbered) in many games, or to hold paints or small bits of other materials.

18. Travel posters, maps. You can get marvelous giant posters, three feet high, from Giant Sized Posters (See list of Sources at end of this book for address and cost information).

Ideas
for Programs and
Service Projects

. . . . Some organizations plunge so quickly into program planning that they forget to put first things first—getting working objectives in mind clearly and checking on them regularly. A thorough reading of Chapter 1 will help your group fix in mind clearly what it is to do and be.

While older adult groups are organized as antidotes to loneliness, they should have in mind other objectives. Older people are still **persons,** who need creative self-expression and who may need to develop a great deal more self-confidence. Certainly they need to feel useful, wanted, needed. Program goals should be set openly and honestly in conjunction with older adults. This should be regular homework.

Many groups plan their programs broadly for the entire year and duplicate them in an **annual program booklet.** Including names, addresses, and telephone numbers of members in the booklet helps the individual's sense of belonging. Group members can help prepare and distribute it.

PROGRAM IDEAS

1. For **parties and banquets**, see Chapter 3; **hobby and craft ideas** are in Chapter 10.

2. **Potluck suppers** are very popular; each person brings a dish.

3. **Speakers.** Many will come with interesting talks, on such subjects as "Social Security," "Behind the Scenes in Radio and TV," "News Gathering," "My Trip to Russia," "Conditions in Our North End," "This Wonderful World." Ministers, rabbis, priests, politicians, professors, social workers, and other professional people (doctors, lawyers, and educators) are often willing to come if asked.

4. **Plant exchange.** Every spring one group encourages members to bring seeds, slips, and plants, with directions for planting. A specialist in gardening (perhaps an older adult) might be on hand to give further instructions.

5. **Movies, travel ideas.** Schools, social agencies, churches, and temples have access to interesting free movies. Oil companies, Greyhound, and the state and federal governments have many films of interest.

6. **Table talk.** For coffee break and teatime, it doesn't take much to get people going. Give plenty of time for visiting.

7. **"Guess the baby."** Let people bring baby pictures and see if they can guess who is what picture.

8. **Book reviews.** They don't have to be formal to be enjoyable.

9. **Window-shopping trip.** If the club meets in a shopping area, the members who wish could go out for an hour, then come back for refreshments to tell of their experiences.

10. **Mad hatters.** In the spring, have a time for the women to show crazy hats, and let the men design some too from materials brought (or have another activity for the men).

11. **Open house.** Once or more a year, have one in which mem-

bers bring visitors to the club for a program, for seeing objects made, photos taken, things done.

12. **Bazaar.** Many groups have one or more a year to raise money and to show handwork that has been done.

13. **Leisure Time Club.** One group has it on Thursdays. Come early and stay as long as you like.

14. **Classes.** Learn sewing; oil, watercolor, and textile painting; leatherwork; tray making; bridge; or how to play a musical instrument, especially the autoharp. (This is so easy that almost everyone can play, since it makes its own chords when you push a button. Many public schools have them now, and you might find music teachers who would instruct. You can buy autoharps through Sears Roebuck and Montgomery Ward, with instruction booklet included.)

15. **Flower growing.** Sometimes in or near the area in which the club is located it is possible to have a little "community" garden for members. Flowers could be used in meetings, for the sick, and in other gracious ways. Many men like to raise flowers.

16. **Wooden game chest.** The men might make the chest for use when no special program has been planned.

17. **Park outings.** See Chapter 9 for some day-camping ideas.

18. **Exhibit of yesteryear.** This could be a program in itself, with the members bringing keepsakes—old books, magazines, papers, clothing, advertisements—and explaining them. It could also be incorporated into any other program of reminiscence.

19. **Birthdays.** Usually they will be celebrated in some special way, but each month, or even each week, the birthdays could be noted and "Happy Birthday" sung to the fortunate.

20. **Tinker table.** One group had a table with odds and ends of material for interested people to "tinker" with. This could lead to a tinker box of material, to a "Dunworkin' Den," where the men could hold forth. For women, the odds and ends could be craft materials, pieces of cloth, or yarn. Sometimes men like to learn to sew, if they can conquer their masculine fright at doing something that women supposedly do.

21. **Bird-watching, bird-feeding.** If the club is properly lo-

cated, it might have a special bird-feeding station. Members who have binoculars bring them to do bird-watching. A good activity for day camp.

22. **Using tape recorder.** Taped programs taken to house-bound members help to recall the joy for those who couldn't be present, and members can give greetings on tape to be taken to those who are homebound, in hospitals, or in rest homes. Likewise, the absent could send messages back to the group.

23. **Thumbnail sketches.** Between meetings, special interviews could be held with members, to be presented at meetings as short thumbnail sketches of interesting facts about the person's past.

24. **Potted plants, window boxes, club pets** (fish or birds). In some circumstances, the care of plants and pets could be interesting.

25. **Gripe session.** Everybody gets his gripes out of his system! In small groups, perhaps. Some like to write out their gripes, then burn them to get rid of them, in symbolic ceremony.

26. **Equipment game program.** If the club has some of the equipment games in this book, just playing them can be an interesting program.

27. **Service projects.** Older adults like to be useful. See the service project section of this chapter for some ideas that may help keep programs interesting for several sessions.

28. **McGuffey's Readers.** Entire programs have been held using these readers as stimulation. They are being printed again.

29. **"Oldsters' dinner."** In Lebanon, Pennsylvania, a full-course dinner was held for the older folks, including Polaroid pictures; each person was given a potted plant.

30. **Spelling bee.** Get an old-fashioned speller, men against the women, or have an old-time turn-down spelling match.

31. **Singing.** Get hymnals, songbooks (such as the wonderful *Let's Sing*, published at one dollar by Transcript Publishing Company, Little Falls, Montana, which has words in enlarged type.

32. **Radio, TV.** Discuss favorite programs.

33. **History.** How this community got the way it is; how this church or synagogue was founded, etc.

34. **"Snip and stitch."** That's what one group called its crocheting crowd.

35. **Stag party** for men only.

36. **Hen party** for women only.

37. **Hobby, putter shop.**

38. **"Men's surprise."** The men are in charge of the program in which they can do anything they please.

39. **"Women's surprise."** Same idea.

40. **Quartets, orchestras.**

41. **Annual hobby show.**

42. **Beautifying the grounds,** wherever the club meets.

43. **Cooking.** Let the men occasionally whip up something to show that they can cook too.

44. **Bookbinding.** If the group is interested, someone from the library could show how.

45. **"We remember"** session, inviting in youngsters to acquaint them with things of the past. Kids these days miss the meeting of the generations. Sometimes they feel rootless. They will enjoy such subjects as school, courting ideas, sleigh riding, candy pulls, and other recreational things older adults did as children.

46. **Polaroid camera.** Just as a tape recorder makes its record of events instantly, so almost does this camera. Some older adult groups are taking advantage of this by taking pictures of the club to send to others and by sending their camera out to absent ones to take pictures to bring back.

47. **Debates,** discussions. These make interesting programs. One group at Thanksgiving time debated whether the season should be an occasion for fasting (women) or feasting (men).

48. **Trips** are suggested in Chapter 9. Use bus, auto, train, plane, boat to get there. Go to fairs, festivals, historic spots, industries, ball games. One group chartered a boat for a special excursion trip. Chartering buses, train coaches, even planes will lead to interesting experiences, if the money can be found. Some

groups also like to go to plays, art exhibits, religious meetings together.

49. **Old photography shop.** One group had fun setting up for people in costumes to pose as for tintypes, representing pictures of yesteryear.

50. **Year 2000.** Sometimes older adults like to look forward too. "What will it be like in the year 2000?" could be an interesting program.

51. **Literary evening.** One group called its program that, giving out poems, jokes, monologues to read. They also allowed members to play the piano and to sing in duets or with the "chorus."

CLEVELAND PUBLIC LIBRARY CLUBS

Using the library as a meeting place, under the direction of Mildred Dorr and Fern Long, the Cleveland Public Library launched five clubs: Book Review Club; Current Affairs Club; Exchange Group; Music Lovers Group; Travel Group. The objectives of the clubs were these:

Book Review Group. To keep up with new books, to gain new knowledge, to discuss together the ideas of books, to exchange friendliness.

Current Affairs Group. To learn things there was not time for when children were little, to make up for missed education, to keep on learning, to keep up with affairs of the moment, to go forward instead of looking to the past.

Exchange Group. To share interests in a friendly group where others are interested in what you have to say, to learn of new things, to keep growing, to have social contacts.

Music Lovers Group. To learn about composers, their lives and times, about instruments and musicians; to understand and appreciate good music; to socialize.

Travel Group. To gain information about new places, people, and ways of doing things; to learn about foreign lands, their history, recent and past; to learn things new, different, unknown.

The Current Affairs Group met for two hours at lunchtime with newspaper and magazine clippings which they read and discussed. Often there were interesting speakers. Each of the groups used materials available in the library. After six months, they had a "graduation," or "Achievement Day," planned by the older adults themselves.

A part of the purpose of the Cleveland project was to get people to fill out a questionnaire on which they gave information about themselves, including the following: sex; age; type of residence; education; amount of leisure time; activities and interests; clubs and organizations belonged to and amount of activity in them; employment, past and present; frequency of visits with family and friends; name, address, and phone number; and any additional information they wish to give the club about themselves.

Other older adult groups may find the development and use of such a questionnaire to be an important way to get acquainted with potential members.

SERVICE PROJECTS

Older adults enjoy not only social and creative recreational opportunities but also the delights of serving others. Through service projects can come a sense of fellowship and usefulness.

Many times older adults have time on their hands as well as useful knowledge and skill in their beings. To many, schooled in the virtue of work, it is not easy to "play." But work for others they like. People can often sing, laugh, joke at their work, with breaks for refreshments and relaxation.

Here are some ideas for service projects which might appeal, given somewhat at random.

1. **Telephoning** to tell of club activities, to cheer people up, to publicize events. Making calls for those who cannot get to the telephone.

2. **Writing letters** for those who cannot, or to people who would appreciate getting mail. Card showers on anniversaries and birthdays.

3. **Reading** to those who cannot read—either the blind or those with limited sight.

4. **Tape recording.** Use the tape recorder to bring cheer to others. Tape speeches, sermons, or programs and take them to others.

5. **Baby-sitting** for members of club, community, or organization. Some might do it in pairs, providing company for each other after the children are asleep.

6. **Helping with the library.** Keeping the library, repairing books, cataloging.

7. **Visiting the lonely,** the shut-ins, those in jail, children's homes, rest homes; giving special care to senile older adults.

8. **Parties for the lonely.** Who are the lonely? Where do they live? Youth or age doesn't make a difference. Nor color. Nor station in life.

9. **Mother's Day for the motherless.** Being substitute mothers or grandmothers.

10. **Others' Day.** Think of them, do for them.

11. **Helping in drives** for money. The more able folks might go from house to house or work as teams with cars.

12. **Driving cars,** taking people who have no transportation. In spring and fall, having color tours to see flowers, flowering trees, fall leaves.

13. **Doing housework** or other chores for a sick person. Cheering up the person by helpfulness.

14. **Baked-goods sale.**

15. **Starvation banquet.** Have a less-than-usual meal but pay full price and send extra money to the needy via CARE, 660 First Ave., New York, New York 10016, or Meals for Millions, 115 W. Seventh, Los Angeles, California 90014.

16. **A covered-dish luncheon** was once held by a church group in the home of a shut-in; the pastor served holy communion.

17. **Sewing costumes** for religious or secular dramas.

18. **Volunteer work** in club, temple, church, community center, office. Helping with mailings.

19. **Raising flowers** for club, church, temple, the sick, hospitals. A cooperative project might be worked out right where the club meets, with garden tools available. Or the flowers could be raised at home and brought to the group.

20. **Raising funds for scholarships,** keeping up with the recipients. This could be done for the United States or for some other country. There are youth everywhere who would like to learn.

21. **Making and selling game chests.** The men could do this. Also woodworking projects to be made and sold.

22. **Clothing scavenger hunt.** Go in cars to homes to gather up clothing to be repaired or turned over to a charity, or distributed by members of the group.

23. **Finding United States host homes** for foreign students studying here. In this plan, a student has a "home" to which he can come for holidays and in which he can get acquainted with American culture. These students might, in turn, provide interesting program material and displays for the club.

24. **Volunteering** to teach skills that are rapidly passing—quilting, crocheting, tatting.

25. **Making** handwork projects for sale.

26. **Sponsoring** a community-wide hobby show—or a hobby show for older adults, especially shut-ins.

27. **Teaching** people how to do crafts.

28. **Keeping scrapbooks,** historical records of the community.

29. **Honoring and encouraging** courageous public officials, local and national. Often good deeds go unnoticed.

30. **Making favors** for banquets, for hospital trays, for children's homes.

31. **Giving** flannelgraph talks.

32. **Organizing** an orchestra or choral group and performing for rest homes, children's homes, jails, club members, and other clubs.

33. **Making and repairing toys** for children, especially at Christmastime, but also all year long.

34. **Beautifying,** landscaping project at club center, not overworking members, but giving them things to do.

35. **Getting out a newssheet,** with additions of original poetry, writing, reminiscences, to send to others.

36. **Being recreation leaders** (volunteer), directing square dancing and the like.

37. **Learning magic,** entertaining groups, especially children.

38. **Storytelling,** especially with children. A storytelling team could visit schools, church schools, and children's homes to entertain and to teach.

39. **Conducting fund-raising enterprises** such as these: having a bazaar, sale, or penny carnival (all shows a penny); making and selling candy, quilts, and rugs (or other sewing projects), woodworked articles, and artificial flowers; raising and selling flowers and plants; buying and reselling articles such as candy and household things; having a spaghetti supper, a pancake supper or breakfast, a smorgasbord, or a kaffeeklatsch; boarding pets during the holidays. See Chapter 10 on crafts and hobbies for other ideas.

40. **Establishing a children's library.**

41. **Giving programs** to bridge the generations—helping the young to understand their own history and what it was like in days gone by.

42. **Collecting and redistributing magazines and books** to persons and institutions who would appreciate them. Mental institutions often like to have magazines for people to leaf through.

43. **Sending holiday greetings** to those who otherwise might not get them.

44. **Holiday food baskets** for the needy.

45. **Playing Santa Claus** to children.

46. **Maintaining interesting bulletin boards** on various subjects.

47. **Pasting pictures** on cards and cutting them up into jigsaw puzzles.

48. **Cooperating** with teachers of young children by making up envelopes of pictures about certain subjects, from magazines and other sources.

49. **Feeding birds in winter,** at the club center.

50. **Making posters** for club and community activities.

51. **Making up collections of sayings and mottoes** for quotation and for bulletin boards.

52. **Home service projects.** See Chapter 13 on fun for home-bound adults.

Parties
and Banquets

. . . . Parties do not necessarily have to last a long time to be enjoyable. It is good to have an interesting theme, colorful decorations, captivating activities, and tasty refreshments, topped with a fellowship closing of some sort.

Older adults generally enjoy having a hand in the planning, which may also include making invitations, mailing out publicity, taking pictures, doing artwork, devising favors, working on decorations. Younger leaders have learned that it is better to have a party **with** older folks than **for** them, if they are at all able to help. If the people are senile, of course, most has to be "put on" for them; in this case, colorful little gifts are particularly good.

A good party has a variety of activities with a change of pace. There may be mixers or group starters, active games, varied group games, mystery or guessing games; drama; skits; music, performed by or for the group; rhythmic activities; refreshments; a closing. There should be time for visiting. The pace may not be as fast as for a younger group. Visiting, reminiscing in the entire group and in small groups is usually enjoyable. Some leaders like to have many creative opportunities for skits, paper-bag puppets, songs, contests. If the group is very large, much may be added by dividing it into smaller groups for games and even work projects.

Don't forget that service projects may bring quite as much enjoyment as parties. Ideas for service projects are given in Chapter 2.

GENERAL PARTIES

Favorite Game Party. Several people suggest their favorite games to be played. Might also include favorite songs.

Circus, Carnival. Devise and put on circus acts—the tightrope walk, animal acts, clowns, etc. Refreshments are popcorn, pink lemonade, and the like.

Blast-Off Party. Imaginary trip to a planet or the moon, with appropriate games, movies, or slides; perhaps the group could even watch the blast-off for some space venture on television.

Back-at-the-Ranch Party. Western idea. Costumes may be constructed of old newspapers or of crepe paper. Put on a "Western," with cowboys, Indians, cowgirls. Trick riding, roping acts, etc., using a broom for a horse. Perhaps a movie or some slides of the West.

Kid Party. Done as things were years ago. Might be the occasion to have people bring pictures of their childhood for "Guess the Baby"—Who is this a picture of, when he or she was a baby?

Storytellers' Convention. A chance to let the men show their abilities at telling tall tales. Might also be the occasion for bringing in someone who knows the history of the community, club, etc.

Gay Nineties Party. With music, costumes, and games representing the 1890's.

Mother Goose Party. Built around costumes, rhymes, quizzes, and music of Mother Goose.

Tasting Party. Everybody cooks—everybody tastes! Blindfold people and see if they can identify ten different tastes.

Birthdays of Famous Men. You could include several, involving those well known locally. Tell of their history and their contributions to society.

Birthday Parties for Members. Many clubs have some monthly birthday recognition, whether there is a special party or not. Cake, candles, and a little present make any heart glad!

Among My Souvenirs Party. Another chance to reminisce in a party setting. Decorate as of yesteryear.

Backwards Party. Everything is backwards. When guests arrive, they are greeted, "Good-bye," then served refreshments. Move right on as if to the beginning. Clothes are worn backwards. Use imagination here.

Hobo Party. Another dress-down party. Newspapers, pins, etc., may be available for making costumes. Storytelling, begging games, "hobo jungle" are ideas.

Pioneer Party. How they did it in the olden days, before the nineties, perhaps. Might be coupled with actual corn shucking or some work project.

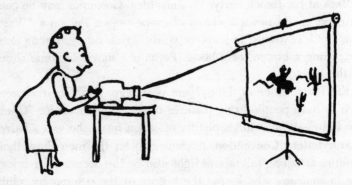

Jet Plane Party. Go in imagination to different parts of the world, assisted by games, movies, slides, posters, and perhaps a speaker.

Arty Party. Let each guest do artwork of some kind and display it, as a part of this party.

Handicrafts Party. In this, the materials are already there, and the time is spent doing handwork—both men and women. If handcraft specialists are available, they might be brought in to assist.

Backyard Party. An outdoor affair in someone's yard, with appropriate games. Equipment games are good—games like horseshoes, badminton, and lawn bowls. Have plenty of seats.

Book Party. A review of good books members have read through the years, with the presentation of favorite parts or characters.

Stunt Night or Variety Show. The older adults might join with others in community, temple, church, or club, or they might do it themselves. Performing is always fun.

Penny Carnival. You pay a penny for each act or event. If many people come, it can be a money-maker.

Equipment Games Party. A pleasant afternoon or evening can be spent playing equipment games such as those listed in Chapter 8.

Sports Party, Splash Party. Go to a sporting event or to the swimming pool. It's fun to get into the water or to sit and watch. Arrange transportation and refreshments.

Poetry Party. Use favorite poetry of members and include the opportunity to write poetry, even put it to music.

Treasure Hunt. Hide a treasure and write out clues, with one clue leading to another until the treasure is found. Can be indoors or outdoors.

PARTIES OF THE MONTH

After-Christmas Clearance. The people bring along unneeded gifts, which they trade or auction to raise money.

Leap-Year Party. The roles of the sexes are reversed, just for fun.

Calendar Party. Hold perhaps in January or December. Do something for each month, perhaps honoring those born in that month.

Cupid Carnival. All bring valentines, which are placed in a valentine box, to be sent to sick members. Carnival games are around the room, for which each person keeps his own score: **Heart Toss:** Each has five fruit-jar rubbers to toss over the necks of pop bottles labeled "Love," "Friendship," "Wealth," etc. **Heart Darts:** Toss darts at a valentinelike heart, marked for points. Adapt other games from the "group" games in Chapter 5.

Washington's Birthday. Perhaps two people could dress like George and Martha. Have a minuet and music a la George Washington's day. Divide into groups to write original stories about "Washington Crossing the Delaware." See Chapter 5 to get ideas for games.

Lincoln's Birthday. Have a committee write an original story of Lincoln's life and act it out. Get Lincoln anecdotes from the library and present them. Lincoln was a lawyer; have a mock court. Use the Gettysburg Address.

St. Patrick's Day, March 17. Irish music, songs, dancing, poetry, and art. This is a good day to invite others to visit the group, for Irish features. Fun idea: "Tell the greenest thing you ever did!" Make Irish costumes with green crepe paper and pins for "Wearin' of the Green." Act out Irish songs. Key words for fun: shamrock, harp, Paddy hat, potato, snake. Tell fortunes with written-out fortunes or a garbed fortune-teller: "The Luck of the Irish"; "Kissing the Blarney Stone."

Mardi Gras Party. Perhaps held on Shrove Tuesday, just before Ash Wednesday. Pancakes are traditional. Costumes, music, noise, acts, and parading. Divide larger group into several smaller ones; let each make costumes from crepe paper, old costume box, etc., and put on a section of the parade or an act.

Mad Hatter's Party, for March. Might be set up as a book party, with features from different books. Alice in Wonderland decorations. Tea as a part of the refreshments.

King April Party. Ardis Stevens, a recreation director in Vermont, had the guests assemble in groups to select a candidate for a king. The candidates were lined up, king chosen. Then there was a queen, and an April Fool. The court marched in and the king and queen were crowned. Groups presented entertainment for the royalty—skits, songs, selections, and recitations. The royalty joined with the commoners to provide some of their own entertainment. **Easter Hat Parade:** Guests are asked to bring a hat in advance. Prizes for the funniest, the most original, the prettiest, and the most becoming. (You might add: the oddest, the most flowery, and the most shocking.)

April Fool Party. With tricks, reminiscences, an April Fool, perhaps adapting ideas from King April Party.

May Flowers. Perhaps a party with lovely music and poetry as "flowers"; or you might get out in cars and go around to see flowers in gardens.

June Travelogue Party. Movies, slides, tales of trips to faraway places.

June Bride Party. Recall when the ladies were brides, whether in June or not.

Patriotic Party for July. Might be outdoors, even attending a community Fourth of July celebration, then coming to the club's meeting place for fellowship, refreshments, and reminiscences.

A **Watermelon Cuttin'** is traditional in some parts of the country. It's mostly sociability with watermelon, but singing, skits, games, and other fun would be appropriate. Make "watermelon teeth" from rinds by cutting up like exaggerated teeth, false-teeth style.

School Days Party, recalling school days, would be fun in September. Set up like old-fashioned school. The program could be recitations, acts, recess; teacher in charge; Parent' Day; graduation.

Halloween Party in October. Don't forget a ghost story, scary stunts, jack-o'-lanterns. This would be a good time to invite guests.

Thanksgiving Party might be held in sections in the homes of different people who cannot get out, or at institutions, becoming a Progressive Party. Transportation would be needed.

Christmas Party also might be either at the club center or "progressive," going from place to place, caroling, taking along presents and Christmas cheer. It might also be worked around making up baskets for needy families, or repairing toys, equipping a Santa Claus, who would go in the name of the group to families or children's homes. Local social agencies might furnish names of needy people. Exchanging inexpensive gifts is always fun. If foreign students are in school near you, they might enjoy a Christmas party with you.

Old-Year Party, at the New Year season, can be interesting. Each person might be advised to bring a letter of advice, written to himself, to put in a box on a table, opened later in the evening and, read. Also there might be the writing of resolutions—"Turning Over a New Leaf." Name tags are "leaves" cut from colored paper. On the back of each is instruction about something to do ("Shake hands with all ladies present"; "Pay compliments to three people," etc.). Gifts might be brought for "Old-Year Gifts," or for "White Elephant Exchange." Sing "Auld Lang Syne."

BANQUETS

Banquets are just parties with food as the main attraction. The table decorations are as important as the room decorations, if not more so. At banquets, speeches of a serious nature are often made, but banquets are still intended to be **social.**

Planning committees for banquets should keep this in mind and do everything possible to encourage people to socialize, even as they arrive and before they sit at the tables. A simple game such as "Who Am I?" might be played, for instance. (See Chapter 4 for this and other mixers.)

Many of the party themes given earlier in this chapter could be transferred right over to banquets, and many program features could be the same. Use your creative imagination, and some good ideas will result!

At the banquet table, after the invocation, the toastmaster might say, "Now look under your plate, find a joke or riddle, and tell it to the people around you." Or there might be a humorous question to ask or discuss.

At banquets people are sometimes asked to move to another location after a course is finished, the ones who move being identified by some favor, or other identification; this helps the entire group to mix and socialize. Sometimes an entire table is asked to lead the whole group in a song appropriate for the occasion or the theme.

The program at a banquet will depend, of course, upon the purpose of the banquet. Decorations may be elaborate or simple —place cards and favors, or none. But to make a banquet memorable, it is nice to provide some kind of souvenir to take home. Some banquets have "head tables," and some do not. Some have music going on during the meal, some have musical performances after the meal, some have group singing. There might even be such fun as the game, "Name That Tune." Some banquets have informal skits, depicting life in the local community or in the club, or just for fun. Some have speeches, quizzes, stories, and the like.

Take a **Birthday Banquet.** There might be one every quarter of the year, honoring those who have had birthdays during the preceding three months. There might be a cake, candles, the song "Happy Birthday," and gift giving, honoring the person for his life and contribution to the club. Some like to have "This Is Your Life," drawing illustrations from the life of the person for the interest (and often the amusement) of the other guests.

"Stars in Your Crown" Banquet. Mrs. Agnes Pylant, who was then director of recreation for the Southern Baptist Convention, told us of a group who had such a banquet for people who had served the church for many years, and were now retiring. The program consisted of speeches, songs, skits to recognize the lives and the long service these people have given in the organization. This idea could, of course, be adapted to a secular group.

Mother-Daughter; Father-Son; Grandmother-Granddaughter. This idea is to show the generations and to honor them, and for older adults this might span two or even three generations! Grandmother-mother-granddaughter, or grandfather-son-grandson, might all be included. The speeches, songs, skits, jokes, recognitions would take into account this unusual theme.

Round-the-World Banquet. This might feature a program by a person who had recently been around the world, or a good film, slides, posters, or other presentations to take the banqueters to other parts of the world. People who lives in other parts of the world might be part of such a program. Often college students from other countries are available to help. Church groups may find missionary presentations appropriate here. Songs, stories, displays from other parts of the world add interest.

Seasonal Banquets: New Year's Day, Valentine's Day, Washington's and Lincoln's Birthdays, St. Patrick's Day, the Fourth of July, Halloween, Thanksgiving, Hanukkah, Christmas. Many of the ideas given in "Parties of the Month," earlier in this chapter, can be used for banquets. You do not even need to feel that people must be tied to the tables if there is room. Also tables can sometimes be cleared of dishes for other activities.

Harvest Banquet. Celebrating the harvest.

Pirate Banquet. Everybody likes to use his imagination to go back to pirate days. The decorations are so colorful.

BEING A TOASTMASTER

The person in charge of a banquet is called the toastmaster. His job is to keep things moving, be in touch with what is going on, and particularly to see that the program is pleasant and of appropriate length.

The toastmaster may want to have his basic meal in advance,

only **appearing** to eat at the banquet. He will have things to organize in his mind, guests to introduce, the program to advance, adjustments to make.

Many toastmasters like to use cards for what they will say, setting aside a card after it is used. If there is a printed program, he may want to check off the items as they are completed.

The toastmaster should have some good humorous material at his disposal, but not be carried away with his own jokes. He is also the "master of **toasts.**" Here are a few:

1. "To every man here. May each be what he thinks himself to be!"
2. "To woman. She needs no eulogy; she speaks for herself."
3. "To the ladies, God bless 'em; may nothing distress them!"
4. "To mothers: the guideposts to heaven."
5. "To friendship: may its lamp be lighted by the oil of sincerity."
6. "Here's to our fellowship—and a full stomach, fine friends, a light heart."
7. "To our nation: one nation, under God, indivisible, with liberty and justice for all."
8. "May we learn to live well and live to learn well."
9. "May we live all the days of our lives."—Swift.
10. "To sunshine and good humor all over the world."

The toastmaster should make sure that he has accurate facts about the people he is to present, especially visiting speakers. If the speaker has the reputation of running too long, the toastmaster should diplomatically try to work out some time limit with him. You as toastmaster may be the only hope of the people!

As well as a good introduction, the toastmaster will want to think ahead about what he will do in conclusion. Sometimes this will be a good story, sometimes a summary of the evening, occasionally a song or a prayer. Whatever it is, help the evening come to a good, clear ending. If the occasion is rather informal, you might say, "Everybody shake hands with fifteen people before you leave the room," after which quick sociability usually begins.

CONUNDRUMS

They are usually "punny," and often the answer is a trick answer which could not possibly be figured out by anyone except the one telling the conundrum. They were especially popular about the turn of the century. Many of these come from a booklet printed at that time.

General Conundrums

1. What is it that lives, but has only one foot? (A leg)
2. What did the man say when he was run over by a steamroller? (Nothing. He just lay there with a long face.)
3. What happened to the housewife who swallowed a spoon? (Couldn't stir!)
4. What did the chicken say about the farmer? ("There goes the guy I'm laying for.")
5. To what man does every man take off his hat? (The barber)
6. What can run but cannot walk? (Water)
7. What did Paul Revere say at the end of his ride? ("Whoa!")
8. What has four legs and flies? (A dead horse)
9. Why did the salt shaker? (Because he saw the spoon holder)
10. What is the difference between the North Pole and the South Pole? (A world of difference)
11. Is life worth living? (Depends upon the liver.)
12. How do you make a Maltese cross? (By pulling its tail)
13. What is it that everybody wants, but never knows when he gets it? (Sleep)
14. What is yours, but is used by others more than by you? (Your name)
15. When someone wants the naked truth, what do you give him? (The bare facts)
16. Why is a false report like a house built on the sand? (Has a weak foundation.)

17. Why does Ireland have such a big population? (Capital is always Dublin.)
18. Where did all the snuff in George Washington's day go to? (No one nose!)
19. What table doesn't have a leg to stand on? (The multiplication table)
20. What is the strong day of the week? (Sunday. The others are weekdays.)
21. What is the unsolvable riddle? (Life. All must give it up.)
22. Name me, and you destroy me. (Silence)
23. What occurs twice in a moment, once in a minute, not at all in a thousand years? (The letter "M")
24. Which has more legs, a horse or no horse? (A horse has four legs; no horse has five.)
25. Why should you never write on an empty stomach? (Because paper is so much more preferable)
26. Up and down, up and down,
    Touching neither sky nor ground. (Pump handle)
27. Why did the sausage roll? (It saw the apple turnover.)
28. What are the biggest ants? (Gi-ants)
29. A man named Bigger marries. Who is bigger? (He. He was always Bigger.)
30. They had a baby. Now who is bigger? (The baby is a little Bigger.)
31. What question cannot be answered "Yes" or "No" without incriminating oneself? ("Are you still beating your wife?")

State Conundrums

1. What did Delaware? (Her New Jersey)
2. What did Tennessee? (He saw what Arkansaw!)
3. What did Ioway? (She weighed a Washington.)
4. What did Mississip? (She sipped her Minnesota.)
5. What did Idaho? (She hoed her Maryland.)
6. Where is Oregone? (She took Oklahom.)
7. Why did Floradie? (She was in Missouri.)

Mixers and Group Starters

. . . . By whatever name, these activities aim at helping people forget their self-consciousness, begin milling around among others, have something to **do**, to use and learn names.

Many of these activities would be quite appropriate for the middle of a social event as well as for the first. The purpose of the mixer-group starter is to get mixing and action.

Some would be appropriate and fun to have before a banquet, if there is enough room.

Assignment Mixer

A. Give a list of ten things to look for in the group, and see who gets through first. Sample list:
   1. Person with mismated sox.
   2. One who has wedding ring on wrong hand.
   3. One whose watch is two hours wrong.
   4. Ones born in December (or other specified month).
   5. Person with two aspirin in pocket/purse.
   6. One wearing glasses that are not his own.

44

7. The one who has been the greatest distance from here.
8. The one with the biggest feet (tape measure handy).
9. The one who has been the lowest down on earth (lowest altitude).
10. Person who is exactly _____ (name the height).

In necessary cases, arrange with individuals in advance to come prepared with clothing changes or other answers to descriptions.

B. Give each one a number and a slip of paper with an assignment. These are just illustrations:

1. Find No. _____ and sing, "Daisy, Daisy."
2. Find No. _____ and together list all the people present who are six feet tall.
3. Find No. _____ and write the names of people who are having a ball!
4. Find No. _____ and convince him that pork chops are not fattening.
5. Find No. _____ and tell him your favorite joke and let him tell one.
6. Find No. _____ and talk about the foods you dislike the most.
7. Find No. _____ and together make a list of people wearing _____ (a color).
8. Find No. _____ and talk about when each of you was first in love.
9. Find No. _____ and tell him what is your favorite toothpaste, and ask what is his.
10. Find No. _____ and find out what is his favorite TV program, and try to convince him that another is just as good.
11. Find No. _____ and talk about how much fun it would be to go to the moon in a rocket.
12. Find No. _____ and swap nursery rhymes.
13. Make up others.

After the mixer is finished, you might ask some of the pairs to perform for the whole group, using their slips of paper.

Group Interviews

This is a superior "get-acquainted" game. Around a small circle (not more than fifteen, less if possible) have people introduce themselves, one at a time, telling where they are from. Then any person in the group may ask the one who has just introduced himself any questions he chooses. (The person may decline to answer if he prefers.) Spend one or two minutes on each person, and you will be surprised at how much you can learn about individuals in the group.

Same Song

Get partners. Have slips of paper paired, with names of familiar songs on them. Each person gets a slip and wanders around the room, humming or singing his song until he finds the other who is humming or singing the same song.

Stand a Minute

Good for any size of group. Let someone keep time with a second-hand watch. At his signal, "Go," everybody stands until he thinks he's stood a minute, then sits. The timer calls out when a minute and five seconds have passed, so each can see for himself how good a judge of minutes he is.

Even or Odd

Each player has ten or fifteen beans. He walks up to someone and asks, "Even or odd?" (meaning the number of beans he has in his closed hand). The person guesses. If he is right, he gets as many beans from the other as he has in his hand. If wrong, he pays a like number of beans. See who gets the most in a given time.

Numbers Mixer

Each person is given a numeral big enough to be seen easily across the room when pinned to him. The leader calls out certain numbers, such as 55. People organize themselves quickly to get several together whose numbers total 55. Each in the first organized group gets a bean for a counter (or a punch on his number). See who gets the most beans or punches. (Instead of sum, the numerals may stand in order to form a given large figure, such as 13,947.)

Face to Face

Persons stand facing partners. One extra calls out, "Face to face!" then, "Back to back!" and finally, "All change!" whereupon they all get new partners, any extras doing the same. Can be combined with "Fancy Handshakes" (see further in this chapter).

In another version, new partners get together, back to back. Then directions are given: "You are a girl who has just seen a mouse. Face to face!" (The women must act out as directed.) Next time, directions may be to a man, "You have just won a boxing match," and so on.

The Borrow Game

Players are seated in a circle. (In a very large group there can be several circles.) Every other player is "odd." When the piano plays chords, each even-numbered person moves counterclockwise around the circle as many position as there were chords, and must introduce himself and borrow from that person some item. Continue until players have accumulated three or four objects, when "REVERSE!" is called out. Each must quickly return borrowed objects, thank donors, and sit down. Last one down pays forfeit. This could, of course, be repeated with the "odds" moving, the "evens" remaining seated.

I've Got Your Number

Give each guest a number, which is to be pinned in a conspicuous place and worn throughout the game. Now provide each person a slip of paper giving different instructions for each, such as the following: "Introduce four to three." "Shake hands with six and seven." "Go to ten and shake hands three ways—Chinese fashion (each shakes his own hand); society grip (hands held high); and good old pump-handle shake." "Kneel before twelve and meow three times." "Find out the color of eleven's eyes." "Ask one what he likes best for breakfast." "Ask two why good men are hard to find." It would simplify matters if odd numbers were given to men and even numbers to women.

Fancy Handshakes (standing)

"We want you to greet the folks near you with special handshakes. Turn to a neighbor and shake hands—"
1. **Pump-Handle Style.** Pump up and down, exaggerated manner.
2. **Fisherman's Style.** Take another person's hand, let hands wiggle backward and forward on push-pull basis.
3. **Model T Ford.** Crank.
4. **Paul Bunyan Style.** The two clasp hands in usual manner, but each grasps his own right thumb with his left hand. Both saw away. Yell "Timberrr!" when the tree is down.
5. **"Hydra-Matic" Style.** Hands just lie in each other without grip. Reason: "No clutch."
6. **Milkmaid Style.** One of the two interlaces fingers of both his or her hands, thumbs pointing up. Turn this combination upside down, exposing thumbs to "milkmaid" (the other person), who hangs on and "milks."

Break the Balloon

As guests arrive, tie a blown-up balloon to everyone's left wrist. Each person must try to keep others from pricking his balloon, while at the same time trying to burst somebody else's. If one or two complete extroverts are in the crowd, this will start—and keep going—with a bang.

Distinguishing Groups

At various parties, guests arriving are given colorful badges to wear. These badges are divided into three or four categories, depending on the number attending. Thus, each guest finds himself belonging to a group for the evening.

Another way of distinguishing between the different groups is to give each group a designated color. On receiving a large sheet of colored paper, each member is told to fashion some type of headpiece.

When the guests are assembled into groups, each group is told to plan a motto, song, and short skit. Thus each group in turn puts on a program for the others.

Birthdays

Everyone is grouped on arrival with others who have birthdays in the same month or quarter of the year as his. The small groups get acquainted and plan a stunt for later in the program.

Guessing Starter

As the people gather, have some of the following ready for immediate attention:

Guess: number of beans in a small glass jar . . . number of seeds in a pumpkin or squash . . . number of peanuts in a glass jar . . . number of kernels on an ear of corn.

Place spices, salt, sugar, tea, coffee, etc., in small sacks, number each, and have guests tell what the sacks contain. (Clue: Sniffing is permitted!)

Hearts

Cut red paper hearts into several irregular pieces and place each heart in an envelope. Number envelopes in pairs—couples work together to mend the hearts. The first couple to mend them wins. (Variation: Cut any symbol, such as Easter egg, Washington's cocked hat, etc., for seasonal emphasis.)

Alphabet Backwards

See which contestant can say the alphabet backwards correctly in the least time. (Use a second-hand watch.)

Longest Peeling

Give each contestant an apple and a paring knife, and see who can make the longest peeling. (Refreshment Stunt: Eat the apples.)

Barbershop

Select two men and two women. Seat both men. Place towels around their necks, barbershop style. Lather their faces with prepared shaving lather or cold cream. The women then have to "shave" their "customers" with teaspoons. The first to do a good clean job wins.

Get-Acquainted Name Game

Give each person a sheet of paper and ask him to write his first (or last) name down the left side of the page, as:

W   Each hunts for people whose
A   names begin with the letters
L   in his own name (in this
T   case, with W-A-L-T-E-R),
E   successively writing their
R   names in order—William,
     Allen, Louise, Tillie, Earl, and Ruth, for example.
     The first to finish his name card wins.

Guessing Weight

Pick out two heavyweights. Let each of these two, in turn, choose six other heavyweights. Place bathroom scales in front of one group and weigh all seven. Do this same thing with the other seven. Add up. The group having the higher total is awarded a package of bubble gum.

Circle Shake

Players form a circle. One person is designated to start by shaking hands with the person to his right, continuing to each person until he reaches his own place. Each person follows the leader—shaking hands and giving his name.

Conversation Mixer

Give out numbers—two 1's, two 2's, and so on. Instruct each person to find the other person who has the same number. Then give out topics of conversation (not too weighty) and have each pair discuss its subject for a given number of minutes. If folks are having a good time, you might then gather and redistribute the numbers and give out another topic.

Song Scramble

Cut up songs into sections and number the pieces of first song, 1, the second, 2, etc. Groups find each other and sing the song.

Who Am I?

As guests arrive, pin names of famous people on their backs. They have to go around to others, asking questions that require a "Yes" or "No" answer until they can guess "who" they are. After they have successfully identified themselves, they may put the name tag on front and wear it through the party. (Variations: "What Am I," "Where Am I.")

"Up, Jenkins!"

5

Group
Games

. . . . The games in this selection are often called "party games." Many of these were sent to us by older adults; all of them are suitable for older adult groups.

In reading the games, especially in preparation for socials, be sure to note and gather the materials needed.

Most of these games could be adapted and renamed. For instance, "Aunt Helen Went Shopping" might be renamed for a member of the group for fun or to honor her. "Bell Pass" could be used at Christmastime. Instead of "Drop the Keys," anything could be dropped that would make a loud noise. In "Flash Cards," there are many categories that could be used. For a Thanksgiving party, it could be "Items that we are thankful for." For Christmas, "Name of a Christmas present."

Sometimes, to make a game fit better, the rules might be modified. The authors consider most of these reasonably "standard" games, proven over and over again to be useful in bringing fun.

Many mixers-group starters (see Chapter 4) would be useful later in the social as well as at the first.

Drop the Keys

The leader greets a player seated in the circle by exchanging names with him, and the two start in opposite directions around the circle, speaking to every fourth or fifth player, who in turn does the same thing. When several are on their feet, the leader suddenly drops a bunch of keys, and all rush for places. The last to find a seat becomes "It" and takes the keys.

Bell Pass

The players stand in a circle and pass a bell (or other noise-maker) through their hands behind their backs. "It" tries to guess who has the bell, and when he succeeds, the person holding the bell becomes "It."

Squirrel in the Tree

Players stand around the room by two's, holding hands to form "trees," with a third (the "nut") in the middle of their little circle. Two or more "squirrels" are trying to get nuts. On a signal called by a squirrel—Nuts!—all nuts must change trees, and each squirrel tries to get a tree too. Those nuts left out become squirrels, and one or all will give signal—"Nuts!"—for a change.

Aunt Helen Went Shopping

This can be done as a performance stunt with five players who come up front, or in a group of not more than twenty.

"My Aunt Helen went shopping, and guess what she bought?" the leader says. "What?" is the answer. "A pencil sharpener," is the reply. Then each person must act out sharpening pencils down the line, for his neighbor, and each action is continued for the duration of the game.

Other things she bought: electric milker (milking motion) . . .
bubble gum (chewing) . . . bicycle (pedaling motion with feet)
. . . spring seat (bounce up and down) . . . cuckoo clock (say,
"Cuckoo, cuckoo") . . . Spinning wheel (rock back and forth).

As a large-group activity, the entire group begin to do the
action as soon as they are told (suitable for auditorium and banquet use).

Going to London

Up to twenty-five players are seated in a circle, and one player
says, "I'm going to London, and I'll take with me an apple."
The next person adds something beginning with "B," and so
on. This is effectively played when a person from the group is
moving to another town; substitute the name of that town for
"London."

Musical Hats

As music plays, three hats are passed around the circle. Each
person must try on each hat as it comes by him, then pass it on.
When the music stops, whoever is wearing a hat pays a forfeit,
counts a point against himself, or is eliminated.

I'm Thinking of a Word

In a group of up to fifty, seated in a circle, a player starts off:
"I'm thinking of a word that rhymes with 'light.'" Others must
guess by acting out a word, such as "sight" or "might." They
ask, "Is it _____?" and then act out the word they think it is.
Whoever guesses correctly becomes "It" for the next time.

In Cahoots

The "accomplice" places his left hand on the leader's right
shoulder and follows him around the room while the leader says,
"The Magic Circle now begins . . ." He repeats this phrase as
he walks until some person speaks. Then he says to the accomplice, "Are you in cahoots?" (meaning "Did you notice who
spoke?"); the accomplice replies, "Yes, I'm in cahoots," and leaves

the room. Then the leader gives a small object to the person who spoke. The accomplice returns and can, of course, identify who has the object. (If the accomplice did not note who spoke, he would have said, "No, I'm not in cahoots.")

Buckets

Seated in a circle, the group learns that each person is to pantomime a bucket on the floor in front of him. Each person, without talking and in turn, shows how high the bucket is, what its other dimensions are, its shape, whether it has a handle. After all have pantomimed their buckets, they pantomime the contents; one at a time, they show, by the way they take the contents out, what it is (or the way they let, say, "beans" run through their hands). Others may be asked to guess what is in the bucket.

Balloon Sweep

Each team of five or six, standing in a circle, has a balloon, some spares, and a broom. At a signal, the first player sweeps the balloon around the circle and back to place with the broom; the next one then does the same, and so on. If a team breaks its balloon, it must blow up another one, tie it, and continue.

Do This and Add Something

The leader, in a circle of not over twenty players, starts some action. The person to his right repeats the leader's action and adds one of his own, and so on around the circle. (Sample: Leader waves hand, next person nods head, third shakes a foot. Actions are done in sequence, one at a time.) If there are more than twenty players, divide into two or more groups.

Clap Out Rhythm

Divide the crowd into several groups. Each of the smaller groups thinks of a song and in turn claps out the rhythm; the larger group has to identify its song title. Could be done on the platform at a meeting or banquet, with the entire group guessing the title.

Button, Button

The players sit in a circle with one player at the center. The players in the circle pass a button back and forth, all keeping their hands in constant motion as if they are receiving or passing the button. The center player tries to guess who has the button. When he does, the player who has it takes his place. (Variation: Pass a thimble or coin.)

Rainbow Game

The colors of the rainbow are, of course, red, orange, yellow, green, blue, indigo, and violet. Starting around the circle, the first person names something red, the next, something orange, and so on. When someone misses, he stands behind his chair. See who can stay in the longest.

This Is My Nose

The group is seated in a circle with "It" in the center. "It" approaches one of the players in the circle, points to his eye, and says, "This is my nose." Before "It" counts ten, the person approached must put his finger on his nose and say, "This is my eye," or else become "It."

Elephant

Group of not over thirty, seated in a circle. "It," in the center, suddenly points to any person, who must make an elephant trunk with both fists. The persons on each side of him must make elephant ears by cupping their hands and placing them at his ears. The last of the three to take care of his responsibility becomes "It."

Cross Questions and Silly Answers

The players sit in two facing rows. One person whispers a question to each player on one side, and another person gives an answer to each player on the other side. The first player on the one side asks his question, and the player opposite gives the answer he was assigned. Since neither of the people who gave out questions and answers knew what the other was doing, you can imagine the results when the questions and answers begin to fall! "What is your name?" asks Number One. "The Battle of Dunkirk," comes the response. "Do you know the height of the highest tree?" asks Number Two. "Blood, sweat, and tears," comes the response.

Pin the Tail on the Donkey

One by one, the players are blindfolded, and try to pin a tail, handed them, on the figure of a donkey that is on the wall. (Can be adapted to other animals and themes, such as pack on Santa's back, arrow on the heart, pole on the flag, or rider on the horse.)

Mother Goose Song

The group is divided into several smaller groups with five to twenty players in each. The leader gives each group one minute to think of all the nursery rhymes they can. Then he leads the entire group in the "A-B-C-D" chorus, after which he quickly points to the group that must sing next, just as the chorus is finished. That group must sing a rhyme to the same tune, such as, "Baa, baa, black sheep . . ." The rule is that no group is permitted to sing a rhyme that has been sung. As the entire group again sings the chorus, feverish behind-the-scenes choices must be made about the next rhyme, for the leader may point to the same group again if he chooses. (This game is often followed by dramatization of one of the rhymes, for the group to identify.)

I Have an Idea

While Jim leaves the room, the group selects a hidden object—a chair, for example. When Jim returns, Sally says, "I have an idea." "What idea?" he asks. "It's just like you," says Sally. "How?" asks Jim. "Has legs," replies Sally. Jim can either have one guess now or wait until clues pile up. Each player tries to give a very veiled clue. Whoever gives the clue that helps Jim guess correctly must leave next time.

Magic Writing (also called Magic Cane, Mysterious Writing, Chinese Writing)

Jane and Martha have worked this one out in advance, and Jane leaves the room. The group picks a word, "basket," for example, for Martha to write with the magic cane (any stick). Jane comes back into the room, and Martha makes many mysterious motions, and says, "Be careful." Then she taps once and says, "Stick to it, gal." Then she makes mysterious curlicues on the rug and says, "Keep your mind on this writing." Then she taps twice and says, "That's all," whereupon Jane says, "The word is 'basket.'" (Key: The first letter of each sentence Martha says gives consonants. The taps give vowels—one tap is A; two is E; three, I; four, O; five, U.) This could be done on a blackboard or curtain with a pointer, at a banquet or for auditorium fun.

Coffeepot

When Tom returns to the room, he finds the group using the word "coffeepot" instead of the hidden word in sentences. He must guess what the hidden word is. (Use words with many meanings, like these: raze, raise, rays; dear, deer; so, sew, sow.)

Black Magic (also has other color names)

When Mrs. Jones returns to the room, Mr. Smith is calling off objects. "Did we choose this?" he asks, pointing to a black pocketbook. "No," she says. "Is it this?" he asks, pointing to a lamp. "Yes," she says, and she's right, because the object will be the first thing following something indicated which is black.

The Organ Grinder Man

While one is out of the room, the group selects something for him to do, such as pick up a paper or play the piano. This is indicated by singing loudly when he is near the object or when he is doing the right thing and softly when he is far from it or not doing the correct action. Song: "The Organ Grinder Man," or one appropriate for the season.

The Guessing Bottle

Ask the "guessing bottle" (a soft-drink or milk bottle) a question that can be answered by its pointing to a person, then spin the bottle in the middle of a circle of players. "Who is the most intelligent person here?" "Who is going to be married next?" "Who is the most beautiful one here?"

Train Trip

Let the crowd choose a conductor, brakeman, newsboy, porter. Arrange chairs, two rows on each side of an aisle, like a train coach. Each of those chosen improvises on his role to make things fun. Every time the conductor calls out a station, those sitting the closest to the aisle move ahead one person, those at the head of the line going to the foot.

This imaginary trip can be altered to fit the Space Age by making it a blast-off for the moon or other related venture.

Shoe Scramble

All of one sex remove their shoes, place them in the center of the floor. The other sex mixes them up. The first person to find, lace, and tie his own shoes is the winner. Repeat for the other sex.

Human Frog Pond

Those with high voices say in fast, screeching tones: "Tomatoes! Tomatoes! Tomatoes!" The altos and tenors say in slower time: "Potatoes! Potatoes! Potatoes!" The low voices say in very slow time: "Fried bacon! Fried bacon! Fried bacon!" Practice separately, then put it all together. This is a favorite of Ethel Bowers, a well-known recreation leader, of Youth Service, Inc. Can also be used for banquets, as a group starter.

What Is It We Have in Mind?

Two people are sent out of the room, and the others agree on some object. It might be the little finger on Mary's hand or the Mississippi River at Memphis or Christopher Columbus or anything else.

Two people are chosen to answer for the group, and the couple are called back and told to ask any questions they wish in order to discover what object the group has agreed upon.

The two who are to answer the questions answer as follows: simply "Yes" or "No" if they can do so; if they do not know how to answer the question, they say "X."

Keep time, and if the answer is not figured out in five minutes, stop the questions and tell what the object is.

What Is It?

One player goes out of the room, and the others select some thing. He returns and tries to discover by questioning what it is; he is allowed twenty questions. He probably will first try to locate it. "Is it in this room?" "Is it in this town?" "Is it inanimate?" When he thinks he has it, he names it. If he is correct, another player, perhaps the one who gave him his cue, goes out and the game continues. If he is wrong and still hasn't used his twenty questions, he proceeds to ask more. This is a great game for a mentally alert group.

Twenty Questions

Similar game to the above, but played with the leader indicating that the object is animal, vegetable, or mineral. Players are limited to twenty questions to discover the object. Questions must be of the type that can be answered "Yes" or "No."

Flash Cards (Letter Cards)

If you get a printer to make some flash cards on cardboard (or make them yourself) you can do much for a group starter. The letters should be large enough to be seen by all. Here are some uses: (1) Tell a story and hold up a letter. The first person who mentions the object called for (name of an automobile beginning with the letter—or a proper name, name of a city, a famous person, famous product, etc.) gets the letter to hold for counting points. (2) Grocery store. Divide the crowd into two sides. When a letter is held up, the first side mentioning some object in a grocery store beginning with that letter, gets a point for his side. (3) Use the idea with biblical characters, things you would see on a nature hike, musical terms, things you would see in a garage, etc.

Up, Jenkins

The players sit in teams on opposite sides of a table. Each team selects a captain. An object (coin, button, pebble, etc.) is given to one team, and its members put their hands beneath the table and pass the object back and forth among themselves. At their captain's command, "Down, Jenkins!" the team that has the object place their hands flat on the top of the table, palms down.

The other side consults awhile and then their captain calls, "Up, Jenkins!" pointing to one hand. The player pointed out must lift his hand and put it under the table. The objective of the opposing side is to guess under which hand the object is located. Then they call all other hands up, one at a time, endeavoring to leave the hand holding the object until last. If the captain of the guessing side happens to call the hand that covers the hidden object, the side in possession scores as many points as there are hands left on the table. No one but the captain may order hands up. Then the object is given to the other side and the game continues.

Blindfold Barnyard

The person who is "It" is blindfolded and given a stick. The players form a circle about him. The blindfolded player goes about the circle and with his wand points to someone. This person must take the end of the wand in his hand and do as the "blind" man directs. "It" tries to recognize by the voice who is at the other end of the wand. He says, "Grunt, pig, grunt," or "Crow, cock, crow," or "Bray, donkey, bray," etc. If "It" names the possessor of the voice, that person becomes "It."

Location

Choose two leaders, who choose up sides. One leader begins by calling the name of some town or place and then counting ten. While he is counting, the opposite person must answer where the place is. If he fails to answer before the count of ten, he must drop out.

Then the leader of the other side takes his turn and challenges some player of the opposite side. The side that stands up the longest wins.

Let It Go

An object (stick, coin, etc.) is placed in the hands of one person in a circle. (If the circle is large, two or three objects can well be used.) The pianist plays; at intervals, he stops playing abruptly. As the music is being played, the objects are being passed from one person to the next. When the music stops, the person or persons caught with the object(s) in their hands drop out. This continues until only one is left.

With Whom You Were, Where You Were, and
What You Were Doing

Three persons go around to those sitting in the circle, one whispering to each person "with whom you were," and second telling them "where you were," and the third telling them "what you were doing." As one does not know what the others are saying, some rare combinations will result.

The players must tell in turn what they have been told in this manner: "Once I was with a policeman on the roof playing 'Ring Around the Rosy.'" In one group, we understand, a very staid old maid got this combination: "I was with the YMCA secretary sitting on the radiator smoking cigarettes."

Bug

Make hexagon-shaped tops with the letter B, H, T, E, L, and F on the six sides. Or use cubes. Supply each player with paper and pencil. A player spins the top. If "B" comes up, he draws the body of the bug and spins again. If he gets an "E" this time, he loses his turn, for there is no head into which to fit the eye. The best second throw, therefore, is "H," for the head. "T" is for tail, "L" for leg, and "F" for feeler. The bug must have two eyes, two feelers, and six legs in addition to its body, tail, and head to be complete. When a player tosses something he already has, he loses his turn. He cannot start drawing his bug until he gets a "B" for body. The first one to complete his bug wins.

Pass the Ring

Players sit in a circle with "It" in the middle. A heavy ring is slipped onto a cord long enough to reach around the circle, and the ends are joined. The ring is passed along the cord from played to player. All keep their hands in motion as though passing the ring. "It" must find the ring. The person he catches with it then becomes "It."

Who's the Leader?

Players sit in circle. One player goes out, and a leader is elected. The whole group starts clapping and continues until the player sent out returns and takes the center of the ring. It is his business to discover who is leading the crowd in its actions. The leader changes from clapping, for instance, to patting his head, twirling his thumbs, rubbing his cheek, etc. All the crowd does the same thing immediately. All players should not watch the leader. It's amazing how quickly the action goes around the circle and how difficult it sometimes is to discover the leader. When finally discovered, the leader goes out and a new leader is selected. A good game to give the timid a chance to develop initiative.

Tell a Story

Select a word—"friendship," for instance. The first player starts a story paragraph beginning with the first letter in that word— "F" in this case: "For many years a family lived in our community . . ." Make it as exciting as you wish.

The next person must take up the story where the first left off, beginning with the second letter of the word—"R" in this case: "Right away the father went to work . . ." and so on to the end of the story. It is best not to select a word such as "assembly" that has two consecutive letters the same. The fun comes as various stages of the story seem conflicting and someone forgets what has gone before. "America" is a good word to use with a small number of people.

Ducks Fly

The leader says, "Ducks fly," and all must immediately wave their arms, because ducks do fly. If he says, "Horses fly," the group doesn't respond because horses don't fly. If he says, "Geese cackle," they all cackle. Sometimes this is played by eliminating the one who does it wrong.

Laugh a Little

The players sit in a circle with a leader in the middle. The leader must be one who laughs heartily and is very quick.

He begins the game by throwing a plain white handkerchief up in the air as high as he can; while it is in the air, everyone must laugh, but the minute it touches the floor, there must be perfect silence. The leader must catch those who are still laughing and send them from the ring. And so the game continues. If there is one who does not laugh when the handkerchief is on the floor, a recognition really is deserved.

O'Grady Says ... Simon Says ...

Almost everybody has played this, which usually amounts to an exercise drill. When the leader says, "O'Grady says, 'Hands on hips,'" all quickly obey. When he gives a command without preceding it with, "O'Grady says" or "Simon says," the group does nothing. Those who make mistakes may drop out, pay a forfeit, or just laugh it off, depending on arrangements. A good exerciser for a group that has been sitting.

O'Grady can also tell a group to move chairs to the walls and useful tasks like that!

Pass It On

The group sits in a circle, and music plays. An object is passed around the circle counterclockwise. When the music stops, whoever is caught with the object must, the next time he receives it, pass it under his left leg, then pass it on. If caught a second time, he must add: pass it around neck. If caught a third time, add: pass it under right leg. If caught a fourth time, add: stand up. If caught a fifth time, add: sit down.

Camouflage

This game helps folks get acquainted with a home or a building. Send them in pairs, with a list: a penny, a red comb, a ring, a plastic toothpaste cap, a bobby pin, a dollar bill, etc. These objects have been "hidden" in various rooms, yet they are in plain sight. The hiding is done by placing them against something of the same shape or color, or in a position that looks so natural that the thing might be overlooked. The penny could be on a brown window sill. The dollar bill might be on a green plant. One player holds the pencil and paper. When an object is discovered, the two get together and write down the location, moving away a little distance to avoid giving it away to another couple. Players do not touch the objects. After ten to fifteen minutes, all get together and compare notes. Declare a winner, if you need to.

Proverbs

There are many uses for proverbs. They can be dramatized, used in quizzes, in games, or even for partner-getting (cut the proverb in two, and let the two partners hunt for each other). Here are a hundred proverbs with which you can devise all kinds of entertainment.

1. Half a loaf is better than none.
2. Blood is thicker than water.
3. The early bird catches the worm.
4. Beggars can't be choosers.

5. Beauty is only skin deep.
6. It takes two to make a bargain.
7. April showers bring May flowers.
8. A watched pot never boils.
9. Too many cooks spoil the broth.
10. A fool and his money are soon parted.
11. Actions speak louder than words.
12. A guilty conscience needs no accuser.
13. Brevity is the soul of wit.
14. Don't cry over spilled milk.
15. Everybody's business is nobody's business.
16. Clothes make the man.
17. Better to be safe than sorry.
18. Practice makes perfect.
19. A bird in the hand is worth two in the bush.
20. Every dog has his day.
21. Two heads are better than one.
22. Make hay while the sun shines.
23. A barking dog never bites.
24. Misery loves company.
25. As the twig is bent, so the tree is inclined.
26. Like father, like son.
27. Spare the rod and spoil the child.
28. Children should be seen and not heard.
29. Let sleeping dogs lie.
30. There's no fool like an old fool.
31. You can't teach an old dog new tricks.
32. One man's meat is another man's poison.
33. Turn about is fair play.
34. Familiarity breeds contempt.
35. Where there's smoke, there's fire.
36. Laugh and grow fat.
37. A little learning is a dangerous thing.
38. You can't have your cake and eat it too.
39. Don't look a gift horse in the mouth.
40. Easy come, easy go.

41. Experience is the best teacher.
42. If wishes were horses, beggars would ride.
43. Still water runs deep.
44. Don't put off until tomorrow what you can do today.
45. Virtue is its own reward.
46. Practice what you preach.
47. The proof of the pudding is in the eating.
48. Don't count your chickens before they're hatched.
49. If at first you don't succeed, try, try again.
50. A miss is as good as a mile.
51. The empty wagon rattles the loudest.
52. Birds of a feather flock together.
53. A rotten apple spoils the whole barrel.
54. A new broom sweeps clean.
55. A penny saved is a penny earned.
56. After the storm comes the calm.
57. Circumstances alter cases.
58. Better late than never.
59. It is too late to lock the barn after the horse is gone.
60. Better to have an empty purse than an empty head.
61. It is never too late to learn.
62. Marry in haste and repent at leisure.
63. The road to hell is paved with good intentions.
64. Honesty is the best policy.
65. A stitch in time saves nine.
66. God helps those who help themselves.
67. Be sure you're right, then go ahead.
68. It's easier said than done.
69. It's an ill wind that blows nobody good.
70. Time and tide wait for no man.
71. Jack of all trades—master of none.
72. Nothing succeeds like success.
73. Every rose has its thorn.
74. Silence is golden.
75. All's fair in love and war.
76. People who live in glass houses shouldn't throw stones.

77. Every cloud has a silver lining.
78. All good things must come to an end.
79. Nothing ventured, nothing gained.
80. Where there's a will, there's a way.
81. You can lead a horse to water, but you can't make him drink.
82. Forewarned is forearmed.
83. Health is better than wealth.
84. He who dances must pay the fiddler.
85. There are two sides to every question.
86. Necessity is the mother of invention.
87. It never rains but that it pours.
88. It's the hit dog that hollers.
89. Two wrongs don't make a right.
90. A man is known by the company he keeps.
91. Out of sight, out of mind.
92. All that glitters is not gold.
93. It takes a thief to catch a thief.
94. Absence makes the heart grow fonder.
95. Rome wasn't built in a day.
96. A rolling stone gathers no moss.
97. Curiosity killed the cat.
98. A friend in need is a friend indeed.
99. An apple a day keeps the doctor away.
100. Don't put all your eggs in one basket.

Shouting Proverbs

Divide the larger group into as many as six smaller groups. Each small group decides on a familiar saying (see above) like "A stitch in time saves nine." Later, one by one, the groups will be asked to shout their proverb in unison. Each person is assigned one word, and their leader says, "One, two, three, go!" On the word "go," all shout their word simultaneously. All other groups try to guess. Later, if necessary, clues can be given—the number of words in the proverb, etc.

Singing Proverbs

Same as above, but each player is assigned one word, and he sings that word over and over to a familiar tune, like "Auld Lang Syne" or "Jingle Bells."

Charades

One of the best of party games, this is enjoyed tremendously by oldsters. Players are divided into two teams, preferably of five to eight, and each team is sent into a different corner of the room. When all are ready, a member of each team goes to a referee and is told a song title, a two-to-four-syllable word, or the name of a city or town. Each then rushes back to his teammates and acts out the phrase or word so that they can guess it. He can only act in pantomime or hold objects. The following are good examples of words and titles used: wonderful (one door full); keystone (key, stone); pasteurized (past your eyes); sunshine (son, shoe shine); "Singing in the Rain"; "Marching Along Together"; "Three Musketeers"; "O Bury Me Not"; "Don't Sit Under the Apple Tree"; "Swing Low, Sweet Chariot"; "Love's Old Sweet Song."

(Variation: Each group determines phrase or word it will act out for other groups to guess. The only clue given is whether it is a word with so many syllables, a book title, etc.)

Act Out Slogans

Have various groups present advertising slogans in brief dramatic skits for the other guests to guess. They may be presented charade fashion.

Getting Partners

Give the slogans to the men and the products to the ladies, one to each person. Have them match up for partners. The leader had better have a master sheet at hand so that he can give hints to the searchers. In some cases, it may be necessary to give more than hints.

That's Your Sentence

Two players are sent from the room, then return, one at a time, to have a secret sentence assigned, such as "Spare the rod and spoil the child" or "Give a man a horse he can ride." The two do not know what each other's hidden sentence is, but the group does.

The two then carry on a long conversation, each hoping to say his hidden sentence without being challenged by his opponent. If the opponent says correctly, "That's your sentence," he wins; if he is wrong, he loses. If any contestant can say his sentence without being challenged by the other, he wins automatically.

6

Quizzes,
Brain Teasers,
and Pencil-and-
Paper Games

. . . . Almost every person likes to see and to show what he knows—also to show his ability to "figure things out." Older adults are no exception.

In using the activities in this chapter, leaders should take some care not to embarrass those who do not know. As one's memory slips, or as he moves into senility, he could experience discomfort.

However, many of these are just fun, and call for little except cooperation with the leader. Many could be used in parties and banquets for an additional dimension of enjoyment.

Do You Know Your Proverbs?

1. Compounds of hydrogen and oxygen in the proportion of two to one that are without visible movement invariably tend to flow with profundity.
2. A body of persons abiding in a domicile of silica combined with metallic oxides should not carelessly project small geologic specimens.
3. Where there is sufficient positive volition, a successful conclusion may usually be expected.
4. Cast a stroke at the propitious moment when the silverwhite metallic substance is of excessive temperature.
5. The customary symbol of regal power does not necessarily indicate desirable mental tranquillity.
6. Each mass of vapory collection suspended in the firmament has an interior decoration of metallic hue.
7. Deviation from the ordinary or common routine of experience is that which gives zest to man's cycle of existence.
8. A short vocal utterance directed toward the individual possessing a high degree of knowledge meets adequately all the needs of the occasion.
9. Unwonted egotism prophesies the speedy effect of the force of gravity.
10. A vessel under optical supervision never reaches a temperature of 212 degrees Fahrenheit.

Answers to: Do You Know Your Proverbs?

1. Still water flows deep.
2. People who live in glass houses should not throw stones.
3. Where there's a will, there's a way.
4. Strike while the iron is hot.
5. Uneasy lies the head that wears the crown.
6. Every cloud has a silver lining.
7. Variety is the spice of life.
8. A word to the wise is sufficient.
9. Pride goeth before a fall.
10. A watched kettle never boils.

The Planets

The sun has nine planets. Unscramble them.

RAMS .... (Mars)

TOPUL .... (Pluto)

UTRANS .... (Saturn)

CRREUMY .... (Mercury)

SEVUN .... (Venus)

THARE .... (Earth)

PRUITEJ .... (Jupiter)

SURUNA .... (Uranus)

PENNETU .... (Neptune)

1. Which is the smallest planet? .... (Mercury)
2. Which is the largest? .... (Jupiter)
3. Which is the farthest from the sun? .... (Pluto)
4. Which has a ring around it? .... (Saturn)
5. Two have two moons. Name one. .... (Mars or Neptune)
6. Which used to be called Earth's twin? .... (Venus)
7. Which is 93 million miles from the sun? .... (Earth)
8. Which is the nearest to the sun? .... (Mercury)

Space Talk

Match the following terms with their definitions.

1. Apogee (E)	A. Measured from point on earth
2. Perigee (C)	B. Force of gravity
3. Orbit (D)	C. Point closest to earth during orbit
4. Revolution (A)	D. Measured from location in space
5. G's (B)	E. Point farthest from earth during orbit

Imaginary Places

Match the imaginary town with the appropriate state.

1. Fountain (C)   A. Mo.
2. Iron (D)   B. Ill.
3. Mighty (A)   C. Penn.
4. Noah's (I)   D. Ore.
5. Yesshew (G)   E. Wash.
6. Wet (E)   F. Tenn.
7. Hittor (H)   G. Kan.
8. Wellor (B)   H. Miss.
9. Ninor (F)   I. Ark.

Who Can

1. Compile the greatest number of words ending in "ion"?
2. Make the longest list of words using the letters in "United States"?
3. Make the longest list of words beginning with "W" and ending with "R"?
4. Write the best ten-word telegram using the letters in "arithmetic" for the beginning of each word?
5. Keep from laughing the longest?
6. Identify the most melodies as they are whistled or sung?
7. Put together a jigsaw puzzle made out of newspaper the quickest? (Cut several identical puzzles.)
8. Tell the funniest gag on himself?
9. Tell the "dumbest" joke?
10. Show his pet trick, or draw the best picture in the dark?

Bang (Counting Game)

Players start counting in turn. When a player gets a number with 7 in it, or one that is a multiple of 7, he must say, "Bang" instead of the number. When the count gets up to 70, the players should say, "Bang—one," "Bang—two," "Bang—three," and so on.

Click and Tomorrow (Counting Game)

Let all stand except one. The one left sitting, selected and instructed beforehand, is to check on the correctness or incorrectness of what the others do.

Beginning with 1, have the group one after the other call out the numbers—1, 2, 3, 4, etc. When 5 or its multiple is reached, the person is not to call that number but say, "Click." When 7 or its multiple is reached, the person is not to call that number but say, "Tomorrow." When a multiple of 5 and 7 is reached, the person is not to call that number but say, "Click-Tomorrow." When one of these multiples is called and its substitute "Click" and/or "Tomorrow" is not used, the group has to start again with 1 and go on, 1, 2, 3, etc., as before. When one calls a number by mistake, he drops out. Try to reach 100!

1	2	3	4	Cl	6	Tom	8	9	Cl
11	12	13	Tom	Cl	16	17	18	19	Cl
Tom	22	23	24	Cl	26	27	Tom	29	Cl
31	32	33	34	Cl-Tom, etc.					

The Moon Is Round

Players sit in circle about the room—any number. You will need one stick—pencil, even an umbrella. Before you start, be sure to clear your throat as if necessary to speak clearly. Begin by ask-

ing the group to watch you and then do the stunt just as you do. Mark on the floor first to the right half way around, then to the left half way round, then to left the other half way round, and as you do this repeat: "The moon is round and has two eyes, and a nose and a mouth and a chin." Then let others try, going from right to left. If the player fails, someone else tries—all the way around. But tell no one of the trick of clearing his throat before starting.

My Ship Goes Sailing

A bench or pillow is placed in the center of the room for persons who fail to load their ships correctly. A small pillow is used for the ship. One player tosses the "ship" to another across the room or circle as he says, "My ship goes sailing." The one catching the pillow asks, "With what is it loaded?" The first player gives a reply. If the cargo begins with the first letter of the sender's surname, all is well and the game continues. When cargo fails to be in accord with that name, the person receiving the "ship" takes his place on the cushion or bench until he catches the idea and is released by someone tossing the pillow to him for another trial.

The fun is over when everyone knows the catch of loading with name-letter. If someone has great trouble, help instead of embarrassing him.

Fifteen Matches

Put down fifteen matches in a row. One player begins at one end and another at the other. Each is privileged to pick up one, two, or three matches in his turn. The object of the game is to force the opponent to take the last match. It sounds simple, but there will be many a miss by those who do not know the trick. To win, of course, the performer must pick up the fourteenth match. To be sure of this, he must get the tenth match. It will be well for him to try to pick up the second, the sixth, the tenth, and the fourteenth matches. If he counts them as they are picked up, he will have no trouble winning, no matter who goes first.

Guess These Slogans

List advertising slogans or hum tunes of commercials and have the guests write in the product advertised. Or they may read aloud the list of slogans.

Poster Slogans

Number the slogans and post them around the room. Each guest will be given a numbered card on which he will identify the various slogans.

1. Keep that schoolgirl complexion. Palmolive Soap.
2. Chases dirt. Old Dutch Cleanser.
3. When it rains it pours. Morton's Salt.
4. Good to the last drop. Maxwell House Coffee.
5. Hasn't scratched yet. Bon Ami.
6. From contented cows. Carnation Milk.
7. They satisfy. Chesterfield Cigarettes.
8. Add others from radio and TV.

Associated Words

Many words are doomed to be associated with other words, as bread and butter; cup and saucer, etc.

Have the players seated in a circle with one in the center. He points to anyone in the circle and gives him the first word with the word "and." He must respond immediately and correctly or take a point against himself. He then speaks to the next player with another word and "and," and so it goes around the circle. Here are some of the words, and you will think of many more:

Adam and — Eve	Thunder and — lightning
Bed and — board	Fine and — dandy
Ham and — eggs	Cash and — carry
Romeo and — Juliet	Cup and — saucer
Stars and — stripes	Tried and — true

Geography

All are seated in a circle with one person standing in the center as leader. He says, "A" and points to some person, who must respond with the name of a country or city or lake, in fact, with anything that might be found on a world map that begins with "A." If he says, for example, "Annapolis," the leader points to another person, who must respond with some place beginning with "S" (last letter of word previously given), and so on. When one fails, he becomes the leader, and the first leader is seated. It's lots of fun but really quite disconcerting sometimes.

The Cook Who Does Not Like Peas

One of the players commences the game by saying to his neighbor, "I have a cook who does not like peas (p's); what will you give her for dinner?"

The person addressed must avoid the letter P in the answer. For instance, it may be artichokes, onions, cabbage, carrots, but not spinach, asparagus, potatoes.

The question goes on among the players. The one who fails to answer correctly is out and, if leader desires, a forfeit may be asked.

Traveling

This is a catch game. The leader says, "I am going to sail (fly, or travel by train or automobile) to _____. I would like to have you go. What will you take?" This question is asked every player. Many different answers are given, but none can go, as they have not answered correctly.

If a player wishes to go, he must take something which commences with the same letter as the initial of his last name. When a player answers correctly, the leader says, "You can go."

What Goes There?

The players are seated around a large table that has no tablecloth. The leader has a basket containing knife, potato, clothespin, apple, pencil, ribbon—in all, as many articles as players.

At a signal the leader requests each one to pass to his right-hand neighbor the object handed to him under the table.

An empty basket is at the side of leader to receive the articles as returned. Then fifteen minutes is given for writing the list of articles passed through the players' hands. Those having the largest and the smallest correct lists are recognized.

What Are You Thinking and Feeling?

Everyone is given paper and a pencil and asked to write down exactly what his thoughts and feelings are at the time. Someone plays soft, emotion-stirring music while the folks write. After ten or fifteen minutes, all are asked to stop writing. Then, in turn, they read what they have written.

Prescriptions

Give each a pencil and a sheet of paper. Have each write his own name at the top of the sheet and fold the paper down over it. Collect them, mix them up, and pass them out again.

Each then writes down some complaint he may be suffering from—ingrown toenails, impacted wisdom tooth, sciatica, etc. Papers are again folded over and are passed along.

Next each writes the name of some well-known person, not necessarily a doctor. Fold over and pass along.

Finally each writes a "prescription" for the ailment. Pass along again, and each reads aloud the sheet he has.

Example: Mary Jones is suffering from swollen tonsils. The town manager prescribes soaking the feet an hour a day in hot Epsom salts.

Character Reading

Have paper and a pencil for each player. Each one mentally selects a person in the room and writes that person's name on the paper, folds it over, and passes it to the person on his left, taking the paper from the person to his right. No one knows the names written on any of the papers. The leader asks questions; each player writes an answer to the questions as they are given, each time folding over the paper and passing it on. When all questions are answered, each person reads the paper he holds. No one, of course, can be flattered or insulted by what is said about him; persons whose names appear might be given their "readings" as souvenirs.

Suggested questions: Who is he? How old do you think he is? What kind of work does he do? How do you think he proposed to his sweetheart? How do you think he should wear his hair? What is his special talent? Do you think he makes friends easily? How many children does he have?

Vacation Truth and Consequences

Give each player a large piece of paper and a pencil. Each writes his own name at the top of the paper, folds it over so that the name cannot be seen, and passes it to the right. Each then writes some fact or event (real or imaginary) pertaining to a vacation trip, then folds the paper and again passes it to the right. Another fact or event is written down, and once more the papers are folded and passed to the right. This procedure may be continued as long as the group or leader desires.

When the papers have gone far enough, they are unfolded, and each player reads the information on the one he holds. (Make sure no one reads the paper bearing his own name.)

A Musical Romance*

The fillers in this story are song titles. Several bars of each composition should be played on the piano as they come in the narrative. Or they may be whistled or hummed. Guests fill them in or call them depending on the method used. Here is the story:

There once lived on "Ye Banks and Braes O Bonnie Doon" a maiden fair by the name of "Annie Laurie." Poverty stalked in Annie's home, and so she had to go to work before her "School Days" were over. Her mother and brother also worked to keep the wolf from the door. In fact, "Everybody Works but Father."

---

* From E. O. Harbin, *The Fun Encyclopedia*, Nashville, copyright 1940, Whitmore and Stone, by permission.

One day while "Coming Thru the Rye" Annie met "Robin Adair." Now Robin had never heard of "I Dreamt That I Dwelt in Marble Halls," but he was a dreamer nevertheless. And so he said to her, "Last Night I Was Dreaming" of you. Won't you "Let Me Call You Sweetheart"?

To Annie this was "The Sweetest Story Ever Told" and she said, " 'O Promise Me' that you will always be true." Robin answered fervently, "I Love You Truly." So they plighted their troth, and one day they were married "At Dawning." Then business called Robin away on a trip way down in "Dixie." He was gone several weeks and Annie felt "Forsaken." Sometimes she would go "Down by the Old Mill Stream" to think things through. She recalled that Robin had seemed loath to go. In fact he said "How Can I Leave Thee?" In her lowest moments she would feel "The Heart Bowed Down."

She remembered that once he had gotten a letter from a girl named "Sylvia." When she asked him "Who is Sylvia?" he had only smiled and said, "La Donna e Mobile" ("Woman is fickle" from Rigoletto). Then he walked off humming, "I Dream of Jeanie with the Light Brown Hair," and that worried her more than ever.

The "Farmer in the Dell" passed about that time and shouted "Why so glum? You should lead 'A Merry Life!' " She smiled back and said nothing. The letter from "Sylvia" had said: "If you ever come 'Way Down Upon the Swanee River,' I hope that 'Then You'll Remember Me.' " How could she be "Calm as the Night" under such circumstances?

But her fears were groundless. Robin came home and he was the same old Robin. He whispered to her "Love's Old Sweet Song," "In the Gloaming," and "Home, Sweet Home" looked good to him.

The days that followed were indeed happy days. Many a time they rowed out on the "Deep River" and sang songs such as "Juanita," "When You and I Were Young, Maggie," "Santa Lucia," and many others.

Every Sunday they went to "The Church in the Wildwood."

Soon a little stranger came into their home and then each evening she crooned, "Lullaby and Goodnight."

Through the days and years that followed they found happiness and prosperity, and thus life moved along "On the Wings of Song" (Mendelssohn).

Adventures in Art

It is desirable to be outdoors for this exercise. Each person is given a piece of blank paper about one foot square and access to a box of colored crayons. Each is asked to draw something, and then, one after the other, to show what he or she has drawn and explain to the others what it is. Then, each picture, after being explained, is clipped to a line stretched between two trees.

Gallery of Famous Paintings and Art Work

Everyone is given a list of the titles listed in the left-hand column below. The objects at the right are on a table. Each person is to look at the objects and try to match them with the titles.

1. "Ruins of China" .... Broken Cup
2. "The Horse Fair" .... Oats
3. "The Hold Up" .... Suspenders
4. "Cain and Abel" .... Cane and bell
5. "The Peace Maker" .... Scissors
6. "Two Perfect Feet" .... Ruler
7. "An Absorbing Subject" .... Blotter
8. "Made To Be Filled" .... Fountain Pen
9. "Can't Be Beat" .... Rubber Egg
10. "Before Lent" .... Umbrella
11. "After Lent" .... Striped Umbrella
                                                E-A-   E-R
12. "A Bad Spell of Weather" .... W-   T-H-
13. "A Modern Letter Carrier" .... Envelope
14. "The Chest Protector" .... Padlock
15. "Relics of the Great" .... Piece of a stove grate

16. "Bust of a Commentator" .... Broken Potato
17. "Something to Adore" .... Hinge
18. "A Bosom Friend" .... Neck tie
19. "Meet of the Hounds" .... Bones
20. "An Unopened Letter" .... Letter O
21. "The Corn Crib" .... Shoe

See how many you can get without help from anyone. When all have finished, the correct answers are read.

Kitchen Shower

A writing game suitable for a kitchen shower. The answers are things used in the kitchen or in furnishing a house.
 1. What a good workman has to rent. Skillet
 2. A vegetable and a conceited dude. Potato masher
 3. A number of mountains. Range
 4. A member of a baseball team. Pitcher
 5. The appearance of being ill. Pail (pale)
 6. A dressing for meats, fish, or pudding and to criticize severely. Saucepan
 7. What an affectionate couple likes to do. Spoon
 8. What a hackdriver used to catch fish. Cabinet (Cabby net)
 9. Worn on the head and a frame for hay. Hat rack
10. A letter of the alphabet and what you are in. Broom
11. A vegetable and a girl's name. Piano (pea Anna)
12. An oriental country. China
13. A common dog and two thousand pounds. (Curtain (cur ton)
14. A conveyance and the best loved. Carpet
15. A section in a hospital and a painter's gown. Wardrobe
16. A lady's garment and the possessive of she. Dresser (dress her)

A Floral Wedding

1. The color of her eyes and her name?   (Black-eyed Susan)
2. Her nationality and appearance?   (American beauty)
3. Her father's name and the pen he used?   (John quill) (jonquil)

4. How did her admirers surround her? (Phlox)
5. What did they think she was? (A daisy)
6. What was her brother's name? (Johnny-jump-up)
7. With what kind of candy did her admirers bribe her brother?
   (Mint)
8. What did her brother throw at them? (Snowballs)
9. The disposition and name of the fortunate young man?
   (Sweet William)
10. To whom did she refer him? (Poppy)
11. What did he do when he proposed? (Aster)
12. What was her object in matrimony? (Marigold)
13. What did he figure would no longer trouble him?
    (Bachelor's buttons)
14. At what time was the wedding? (Four-o'clock)
15. Who performed the ceremony? (Jack-in-the-pulpit)
16. What officer acted as best man? (Marechal Niel)
17. What did the bride wear on her head? (Bridal wreath)
18. What music was played during the ceremony? (Narcissus)
19. What did she lift to him immediately after the ceremony?
    (Tulips)
20. What did she say as they left the old home? (Forget-me-not)
21. What did they leave behind them? (Bleeding hearts)
22. To what poor fellow did they give the job of houseman?
    (Ragged Robin)

Familiar Trees

1. Well-groomed .... Spruce
2. Sandy shore .... Beach
3. To waste away (with grief) .... Willow
4. Something to keep us warm .... Fir
5. Found in the calendar .... Date
6. An officer of the church .... Elder
7. A game plus a vegetarian food .... Chestnut

Telegrams

Take any name you wish, such as Christmas, Washington (for a patriotic party), etc. Let each person have a sheet of paper headed by the chosen name or word. Set a certain length of time and in that time each one must write a telegram each word of which begins with the corresponding letter in the name. All telegrams must be read aloud with two people chosen to select the best telegrams.

Similes

Similes are simply picturesque phrases likening one thing or action to another. Examples: "As easy as falling off a log," or "As pretty as a picture." The other examples given below are all in popular usage, and you should be able to complete all or most of them. Can you?

1. As rich as _____ Midas (or Croesus)
2. As poor as _____ a church mouse
3. As sure as _____ and _____ death—taxes
4. As smooth as _____ silk
5. As naked as a _____ _____ newborn babe
6. As black as _____ pitch
7. As red as a _____ lobster
8. As green as _____ grass
9. As brown as a _____ berry
10. As free as the _____ air
11. As bright as a new _____ penny
12. As drunk as a _____ lord
13. As close as _____ and _____ one—two
14. As busy as a _____ _____
    _____ _____ with the _____ one-armed paper hanger—hives
15. As slow as _____ molasses
16. As quick as you can say _____ _____ Jack Robinson
17. As happy as a _____ lark
18. As mad as a _____ _____ wet hen
19. As sly as a _____ fox
20. As pale as a _____ ghost
21. As strong as an _____ ox
22. As deaf as a _____ stone (or post)
23. As blind as a _____ bat
24. As plain as the _____ on your _____ nose—face
25. As stubborn as a _____ mule
26. An appetite like a _____ horse
27. A memory like an _____ elephant

28. As meek as a _____   lamb
29. As quiet as a _____   mouse
30. As straight as an _____   arrow
31. As hot as _____   Hades
32. As slippery as an _____   eel
33. As ugly as _____   sin
34. As cute as a _____   trick
35. Drinks like a _____   fish
36. As tight as a _____   drum
37. As crazy as a _____   loon
38. As sick as a _____   dog
39. As thin as a _____   rail
40. As fat as a _____   pig

A Floral Love Story (A variation of the preceding one)

1. Her name and the color of her hair? (Marigold)
2. Her brother's name and what he wrote it with? (Jonquil)
3. Her brother's favorite musical instrument? (Trumpet)
4. With what did his father punish him when he played his trumpet too loudly? (Goldenrod)
5. What did the boy do? (Balsam)
6. At what time did his father awaken him? (Four-o'clock)
7. What office did his father hold in the church? (Elder)
8. What did Marigold call her sweetheart? (Sweet William)
9. What being single did he lose? (Bachelor's button)
10. What did he do when he proposed? (Aster)
11. What did he lay at her feet? (Bleeding heart)
12. What did she give him in return? (Heartsease)
13. What flower did he cultivate? (Tulips)
14. To whom did she refer him? (Poppy)
15. Who married them? (Jack-in-the-pulpit)
16. When he went away what did she say to him? (Forget-me-not)
17. With what did she punish her children? (Lady's slipper)
18. What hallowed their last days? (Sweet peas)

Jumbled Birds

1. GALEE	(Eagle)	6. RITPRADGE	(Partridge)
2. VOED	(Dove)	7. AECPOKC	(Peacock)
3. VAENR	(Raven)	8. LOW	(Owl)
4. WOARSPR	(Sparrow)	9. COTSRHI	(Ostrich)
5. LQIUA	(Quail)	10. NALCIPE	(Pelican)

Words Into Flowers (This one's tricky.)

Add two letters to each; rearrange to make the name of a flower.

1.	SCAT	(Cactus)	6. TOIL (Violet)
2.	PEN	(Peony)	7. LOP (Phlox)
3.	PIT	(Tulip)	8. MOSS (Cosmos)
4.	OURS	(Crocus)	9. SAD (Daisy)
5.	NINA	(Zinnia)	10. RAT (Aster)

Company's Coming

Answer each with an appropriate kind of cake.

1. Drink out of this—Cup-cake.

2. Satan's supper—Devil's food cake.

3. Breakfast beverage—coffee cake.

4. Use this in the bathtub—Sponge cake.

5. Heavenly fare—Angel cake.

6. Stands on its head—Upside-down cake.

7. Sixteen ounces—Pound cake.

8. A child's plaything—Marble cake.

Jumbled Cities

Give each person a pencil and a sheet of paper on which is typed the following:

1. ETELALHSASA
2. RACOI
3. OKESANP
4. AEIOUSBNSRE
5. SOOL
6. AIMDDR
7. HAGISANH
8. TOMLANER
9. OYAMBB

Explain that each is a jumble of the letters which, properly arranged, spell the name of a city, most of them in a country other than our own.

Ask the group to put each jumble in order, so as to spell out the cities. After eight minutes, call for the highest scores.

For the leader's information, the names of the cities are listed here:

1. Tallahassee
2. Cairo
3. Spokane
4. Buenos Aires
5. Oslo
6. Madrid
7. Shanghai
8. Montreal
9. Bombay

Find the Nuts

1.	Dairy product	(Butternut)
2.	A vegetable	(Peanut)
3.	A country	(Brazil nut)
4.	A girl's name	(Hazel nut)
5.	A structure	(Walnut)
6.	Nickname of a president	(Hickory nut)
7.	Every ocean has at least one	(Beechnut)
8.	Every person has one	(Chestnut)
9.	Names of two boys	(Filbert)
10.	Letter of the alphabet and an article of tin	(Pecan)
11.	A beverage	(Coconut)

Aw, Nuts!

1.	What nut is a sandy shore?	(Beechnut)
2.	What nut is a girl's name?	(Hazelnut)
3.	What nut is a stone fence?	(Walnut)
4.	What nut is a large strong box?	(Chestnut)
5.	What nut is one of a country?	(Brazilnut)
6.	What nut made quite a hit with our soldiers?	(Doughnut)
7.	What nut is a vegetable?	(Peanut)
8.	What nut is good for a bad boy?	(Hickory nut)
9.	What nut is an oft-told tale?	(Chestnut)
10.	What nut ought to go fine with hot biscuits?	(Butternut)
11.	What nut is a favorite in Ohio?	(Buckeye)

Active Games

. . . . These games provide for a certain amount of physical activity, and the leader should be careful not to use them with the wrong people. While most of these games are not very active, heart patients should not participate in many of them. If the leader is really convinced that a person should not participate, he should not hesitate even to bring a bit of pressure.

However, older people do need exercise, and people in good health can do all these and more. Some of the group games in Chapter 5 are quite as active as these, as are some of the outdoor events suggested in Chapter 9.

Balloon Race 1

Like the old potato race, a balloon race is a scream. Give contestants inflated balloons and start them for a given point. The balloons may be kicked or batted or treated in any way to get them over the goal, except they **may not be carried.**

Balloon Race 2

Four persons take part, in pairs. Use six to eight balloons about sixteen or eighteen inches long for each couple. The two couples stand in a line, and one of the partners of each couple is given the balloons to place in her partner's arms. When the signal is given to start, the race to reach a given goal begins. If a balloon is dropped, the partner with empty arms must replace it in her partner's arms.

Balloon Volleyball

This game is played with an inflated balloon instead of a volleyball. For a net use a string, rope, or tape mounted between the front rows of chairs. Probably not more than two rows of chairs on each side of the net should be used. The players must sit in their chairs, for they lose the point if they get up to hit the balloon.

Team A serves the balloon by hitting it over the "net." The other team must hit it back in three tries or they lose the point. As in volleyball, outside lines are marked off, and a team wins points only when it is serving. The team first making fifteen points wins (or designate another total goal).

Balloon Basketball

Have two facing lines of players seated in chairs four to five feet apart. At each end is a "goalie," who forms a goal with arms rounded, hands together like a hoop. Or a large basket may be at each end, held at an angle to receive the balloon.

One team decides to knock the balloon up the room toward its goal, the other down the room toward its goal. At least one person is behind each line to recover any balloon out of the control of the line.

Start by a toss-up of the balloon in the middle. Players then try to bat it up or down the line toward their respective goals. Each goal made counts two points. Players foul if they rise from their seats. Play for a specific period of time.

(This is an exciting game, so exercise caution not to play too long or too furiously.)

Post Office

Each player is named for a city. The postman says, "I have a letter from New York to Des Moines." These two players must exchange seats, and "It" tries to get a seat. "Special Delivery" is the signal for all to change. Likewise, this idea has been used with automobiles, airplanes, etc.

Alphabet Race

This active game can use as few as twelve players, six on a team, or as many as fifty-two, twenty-six on a team. Give large alphabet cards to each player, the same letters to each of two sides. Words are called out, and players line up to spell the words properly for the judges or audience. The first team finishing the word, properly spelled, gets one point. Double letters are represented by swinging the letter from side to side.

Here are words **for teams of six players each:** face . . . faced . . . dab . . . feed . . . cafe . . . abed . . . dead . . . ebb . . . beef . . . fade . . . bad . . . add . . . Abe . . . bee . . . . . . bed . . . fee . . . cad . . . deaf . . . bead.

For teams of nine players each: chafed . . . head . . . fig . . . chief . . . cage . . . faced . . . hide . . . chide . . . aged . . . dig . . . dice . . . caddie . . . each . . . beg . . . beach . . . fagged . . . deaf . . . die . . . abide . . . gibe.

For teams of twelve players each: bold . . . cabin . . . blame . . . flinch . . . holding . . . mail . . . dance . . . mailed . . . lambkin . . . gladden . . . bean . . . clock . . . jammed . . . killed . . . gone . . . docile . . . loading.

Involving the entire alphabet: foxy . . . quickly . . . quavering . . . nervous . . . social . . . horizon . . . education . . . puzzle . . . paintbrush . . . doxology . . . scrapped . . . juicy . . . shocked . . . urgent . . . weaver . . . zebra . . . womanly . . . family . . . children . . . lockstep.

Magazine Race (Use With Caution)

Three persons begin on one side of the room and three on the other. (Pick folks who don't mind bending.) Each person is given two magazines, and at a signal, they proceed as follows: step on one magazine, throw the other in front of self, pick up the one just stepped off of, throw it in front of self, etc. If any one of the six persons steps off a magazine onto the floor, he drops out of the game. The side that successfully gets three, two, or one across the room first wins.

Fanning-the-Ball Race

Choose twelve people, or let twelve volunteer. Give each a fan and a ball of crushed tissue paper. The participants line up and place the tissue balls on the floor, the signal is given to start, and each fans his ball across the goal, which is a line about twenty to twenty-four feet from the starting line.

Going to Jerusalem

Set up a row of chairs which alternately face opposite directions, being sure to have fewer chairs than players. The players march around the chairs while music is played. When the music stops, all try to get a seat. The ones left out have to leave the game. One chair is taken away each time. This goes on until one chair remains. The one who gets this seat "gets to Jerusalem." (Caution: Players are instructed to walk, not run.)

Come Along

The players stand in a circle, right hands in toward the center. "It" trots around the center, takes a hand, and says, "Come along." That person in turn takes another one, and this continues until the chain is several persons long. The leader says, "Go home," and all scramble for places. The loser for a vacant place becomes "It."

Mock Track and Field Meet

Advance publicity helps build up enthusiasm for this occasion. If possible, divide into sides in advance, making certain that there are equal numbers of men and women on each team; allow each group to elect captains. Give each team a list of events and let them assign various players to specific events. However, don't tell the true nature of the event.

If the group is extremely large, provide roles on each team for cheerleaders, bands, doctor and nurse, homecoming "king" and "queen" (usually a man is the "queen" and a woman the "king"). Try to get everyone into the act. Encourage cheerleaders and team captains to keep enthusiasm high.

50-Yard Dash (request the fastest man on each team): The first to thread a needle and take 50 stitches on a piece of cloth wins.
Javelin Throw (a man and a woman from each team): Throw soda straw or feather for distance. Variation: Throw for accuracy at large bull's-eye drawn on the floor.
Discus Throw (one man and one woman from each team): Sail paper plate or powder puff as far as possible.
Hurdles (one woman from each team): Peanuts in shell sprinkled along each course. Peanuts must be shelled and eaten as they are picked up.
Standing Broad Grin (one man and one woman from each team): Measure grins and allow one man and one woman as winners. Prize is lemon or ripe persimmon.
Boardinghouse Reach (a man from each team): Measure arm spread from fingertip to fingertip.

440-Yard Relay (two men and two women from each team): Push penny across yardstick with toothpick held in teeth. Run it relay fashion.

High Jump (one man and one woman from each team): Contestants with hands tied behind backs jump for suspended doughnut. Tie doughnuts six inches over head of each participant.

Hammer Throw (one man and one woman from each team): Inflate paper bag and tie with string three feet long. Contestants hold loose end of string, whirl bag around head, and throw.

Shot Put (one man and one woman from each team): Contestants throw balloon or ball of cotton as far as possible. Variation: Contestant singing highest note wins.

Mile Relay (four men and four women from each team): Each team has a ball of twine. The first man holds end of twine and unwraps ball, passing it around himself once. He then passes it to the next player, and so on down the line. The last man begins to rewind string and starts it back up the line. The first team to rewrap its ball of twine wins.

Low Jump (two women and two men from each team): Contestants pass under a string without touching it. Start at three feet and move it down. Touching the string disqualifies a contestant. It is surprising how low some can get!

Two-Mile Race (the man with the biggest feet from each team): Contestants heel and toe around course. The first one to complete the circuit wins.

Flower Garden

Similar to Fruit Basket. Players are given flower names, and "Poison ivy" signals everybody change.

Fruit Basket

Seated in a circle, the players are numbered off by fours. Number ones are lemons, number twos are oranges, number threes, apples, and number fours, bananas. "It" names two fruits, who immediately change places, and he tries to get a vacant place. "Fruit basket upset" is a signal for all to change places. Whoever is left out becomes "It." (In this and the next two games, avoid too much speed in exchanging places.)

Dollar, Dollar

Players sit or stand in a circle, one in the center who closes his eyes until he counts to ten. Players start a coin around the circle and keep it going while they sing. To give them the chance to pass the coin around they clasp hands together (count one) and then move them apart toward neighbor's hands and join for an instant (count two), keeping up this rhythm. The person in the center tries to find who has the coin. If anyone drops it or gets caught with it, he has to exchange places with the center person.

Dol-lar, dol-lar, how you wan-der, from the one hand to the oth-er;

(poor Ma-ry)
Is it fair, is it fair, To keep (Mrs. Jones) stand-ing there?

Stagecoach

Players are given the parts of a coach—spoke, axle, door, lantern, etc. "It" begins telling a story. Suddenly he says, ". . . and the stagecoach turned over," and all must rush to change seats. The one unsuccessful at getting a seat is "It."

RELAYS

Pillow Race

Form two lines with any number of persons participating. Give each head person a pillow and pillowcase. He puts the pillow-

case on the pillow and passes it to the next person, who takes
the case off and passes pillow and case to next one, and on
the game goes until the pillow and case reach the end of the
line. The side finishing first wins.

Broom Hockey

You will need two chairs for goals, two brooms or broomsticks,
and one old (knotted) rag. Form two teams, who sit facing each
other in long, equal lines; the broomsticks lie on two chairs on
each end, and the rag is on the floor in middle. Teams are
numbered from opposite ends.

The leader calls a number, such as "two." The players numbered "two" go to their goals, each gets his broom and attempts
to make a goal by sweeping the rag under the chair of the other
player. If he succeeds, he scores a goal for his team. Then the
rag is placed in the center of the space between chairs, brooms
are replaced, and another number is called. This continues until
all have played.

Use this game with some care.

Circle Relay

Players may sit in chairs, but do not necessarily have to. Form
teams of equal number; each team makes a circle. The first man
gets up and runs around the circle. He may walk, hop, and skip,
to music. When he sits in his old place, the person on his left
gets up and goes around the circle. This continues until the last
person has finished his round.

Variation: Group seated on the floor in tight circle back to
back with legs spread wide, alongside legs of persons next to
them. Each person gets up and hops around the circle between
the legs of teammates and back to place.

Handshaking Relay

Teams are paired, in file formation, with the heads of the teams
facing each other. The first player runs across the room and

shakes hands with everyone in the opposite line. He returns and tags the second player, who repeats the action. Continue this action until the entire team finishes.

Variation: Different types of handshakes may be used for each member of the team. These are explained in Chapter 4.

Tug of War

One player from each team is paired with one from another team. A string three feet long has a marshmallow strung in the middle. Contestant holds one end in his mouth, and the first one to chew up the string and reach the marshmallow wins.

Marathon Race

Use all players from each team. Give each one a peanut. They then push peanuts across the room with their noses.

Handful Relay

The first player is given a handful of objects, which are to be passed, one at a time, and returned. The first team finishing wins.

Grapefruit Relay

Have a grapefruit for each head person. That person fixes the grapefruit under his chin and passes it on to the next person without using hands, turning heads sidewise. The first team getting its grapefruit to the end person wins. Fun for adults, especially those with several chins.

Santa Claus Relay

The first player runs up to a box or chair containing several packages and a Christmas stocking, stuffs the stocking with the packages, empties it, and returns to the rear of the line. Each player repeats the action, and the first team finishing wins.

Broken Car Relay

Each player has a role. No. 1 is a woman driver, No. 2 has water in gas, No. 3 has a flat tire, No. 4 has a broken steering wheel, No. 5 has a dead battery, No. 7 has water in spark plugs, and No. 8 is normal. No. 1 runs up to goal and back in spurts. No. 2 takes two steps forward and one backward. No. 3 hops or limps to goal and back. No. 4 wanders around in a wavery course. No. 5 is pushed by No. 6. No. 7 goes up backwards, and No. 8 runs up and back as fast as possible. Other ideas could be devised.

Equipment
Games*

.... The equipment you purchased will, of course, depend upon the group's interests. Many groups have found these things useful:

1. Tables in general for playing, writing, working.
2. Table games like checkers, chess, Chinese checkers, Carroms, Scrabble, cards, Monopoly, and the Milton Parker games. These are often kept in a game chest or game closet. Perhaps one or more of the men could build the game chest as a project.
3. Paper for letter writing at tables. Telephone for communication.
4. Hobby craft material and space, including a darkroom.
5. Audio-visual equipment: tape recorder, record player and records, slide and movie projectors, television set, opaque projector for postcards.

---

* Check the list of Sources at the end of this book for suppliers.

6. Piano, organ, other musical instruments.

7. Purchased equipment for such games as indoor horseshoes, carpet bowls, bocce, indoor shuffleboard, quoits, croquet, tether ball, beanbags, golf sets, badminton, table tennis. One of the most complete suppliers is **Recreational Research Institute, Inc.,** 258 Broadway, New York, N. Y. 10007, who have a free catalog also showing outdoor equipment. Also **World-Wide Games,** Delaware, Ohio 43015.

8. Outdoor equipment for horseshoes, lawn bowls, croquet, golf, Tamburelli, darts, golf putters, playground, beach balls; camping equipment, outdoor shuffleboard, garden tools, quilting frames, woodworking equipment.

9. Articles members could bring for use, such as cameras, slides, cooking equipment, hobby materials, automobiles, literature for handcraftsmen and for stamp and coin collectors.

Equipment Games Party

Using equipment mentioned above, and games suggested in this section, have an equipment games party! Invite other persons or groups, including people of other ages. Play may be by individuals, pairs, or teams, with tally sheets to record games played and scores. Scoring is finally not so important as the fun and fellowship. Have a good long refreshment period for comparing notes. Close with singing, possibly devotions if a church group.

SOME GAMES INVOLVING EQUIPMENT

Shuffleboard

The size of the scoring areas and distance between them can be varied to accommodate the space available. The playing surface is marked off with paint or enamel. The court (Fig. 1) can be made attractive by the use of contrasting colors for the numbers, lines, and 10-off areas. Make the scoring areas green, the 10-off areas red, the lines black, and the numbers white on black.

Cue heads and disks can be made from two orange or lemon crate ends glued together one on top of the other to get the re-

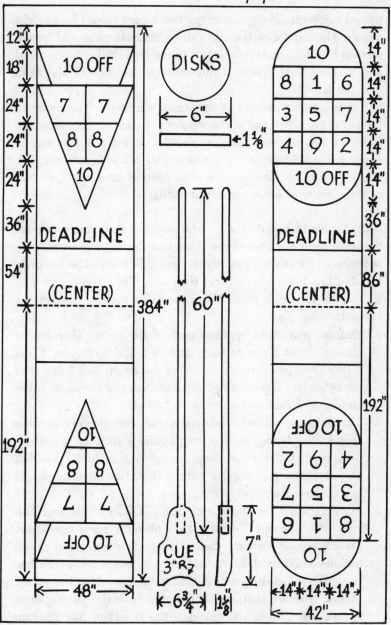

Fig. 1   Fig. 2

quired thickness. The grain of the two pieces should be at right angles. The handle of the cue can be made from an old broom or mop handle. The handle is put in the hole drilled in the head and a round-head screw is put through one side of the head into the handle.

A hole 1 inch wide and ⅛ inch deep is drilled in the center of the top of each disk and in the top sides of each of the cue heads. For each set, the holes are enameled a different color, usually black and red. There are two cues and six disks for each set. The whole pieces are then given several coats of linseed oil, or two or three coats of clear varnish or shellac.

Rules for Shuffleboard: The general object of the game is to push the disks from one end of the court into the scoring area at the opposite end to obtain the highest possible score. The six disks are shot first from one end and then from the other.

1. Two or four can play. The same rules apply for single or partnership play.
2. Partners play from opposite ends of the court. Therefore if players 1 and 3 are partners against 2 and 4, players 1 and 2 take their position at one end of the court, and 3 and 4 at the other end. Partners use disks and cues of the same color. Six disks of each color are used.
3. The disks are pushed or shoved with a cue. If a player steps out of the playing area when pushing a disk, or if his cue goes beyond the 10-off area, he commits a foul. The disk played is then dead for that inning. Disks that are dead should be removed from the playing area.
4. Player 1 starts the game with one black disk. Player 2 follows with one red disk, and then player 1 plays one again. They continue shoving their disks in this order until each has played his six disks. A disk that does not pass the deadline is considered dead for that inning (or period within which twelve disks are shot) and is removed from the playing area. A disk that passes over the deadline is left in that position for the remainder of the inning.

5. The object of the game is to shove the disks into the sections with the highest numbers. The points are added at the end of each inning, credit being given for the position of the disks at that time. It is permissible to hit and move any disk with a played disk. A disk hit and moved during a play is given the value of the area in which it rests at the end of the inning. If a disk is on a line or partially in an area with a larger number, the player receives credit for the larger number. If a disk is on the 10-off line or in the 10-off area, 10 points are deducted from the total score for the inning. A disk that is not on a numbered area does not count in the scoring.

6. After players 1 and 2 have finished shooting, the points are counted and the inning is ended. Players 3 and 4 at the opposite end of the court play the second inning from that end, returning the disks to the first end. The game is won by the team that first obtains a previously determined number of points. The number can be determined by the ability and skill of the players. As a rule, a game is usually 51 points. Sometimes a game is limited to a certain number of innings and the team having the higher score at the end of those innings wins.

7. If only two play the game, both players shoot their disks from one court and count their score; then each retrieves his disks and shoots them back.

Rules for Sequence Shuffleboard: The object of Sequence Shuffleboard is to place the disks, shoving them with the cue, so that they come to rest in numerical sequence on the numbered sections of the scoring area from 1 to 10 and back to 1. It must be played on a court similar to that shown in Fig. 2.

Disks count if they are in sequence at the end of the inning, regardless of the order in which they are placed. Each partner takes up where the other left off. Thus, if player 1 places disks on 1, 2, 3, and 6, the 6 will not count, since it is not in sequence, and player 3, his partner, will begin trying to place disks on 4. If, at the end of an inning, a disk is on the 10-off area, the last number in sequence does not count. Thus, if player 1 places disks on 1, 2, 3, and 10-off, the 3 will not count and his partner must begin at 3 rather than 4. The team wins which first completes the placing of the disks in sequence on the numbered areas from 1 to 10 and from 10 back to 1.

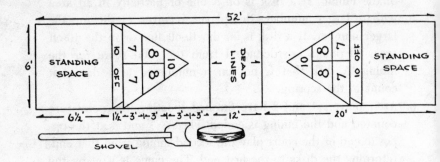

Shuffleboard in Small Space

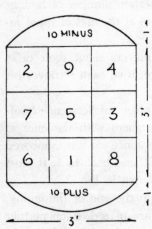

In a space that did not permit regulation shuffleboard a leader soon had thirty-two people playing a modified version of the game. He had chalk, a piece of beaverboard 1 by 3 feet, and another piece the same size with ends rounded. Using the beaverboard, he soon had four courts marked off on the floor. He placed the rectangular piece of beaverboard on the floor and marked around it, then moved it down and marked again. The third time he marked off the lower end of the rectangle (the 6-1-8 section). Then he used it to mark the crosslines, thus dividing the rectangle into nine squares. After that, he used the rounded piece of beaverboard to mark off the ends for the 10 plus and 10 minus. Eight people played at each game, four on a side. All players played from the same end of the court, thus making only one diagram per game necessary. All shovels and disks were half the regulation size.

Table Caroms

Mark a spot at the center of a table (a chalk mark or a stamp). Each player is provided two checkers. (There should be an even number of reds and blacks.) The blacks play first. One of their players flips his checker, trying to land it on or near the marked spot. Then one of the opponents flips a red checker. If the black has landed near the spot, the red player tries to knock the black away. So it continues until each player has flipped both his checkers. Then the side with a checker nearest the target earns one point. It also gets a point for every other checker that is nearer the center than any of the opponents'.

Table Shuffleboard

On a table make a beaverboard shuffleboard five to six feet long, with a backboard an inch high to stop the disks, which are checkers. The players flip them by shooting with the forefinger. The same diagram (in miniature) is used as a regulation shuffleboard, and play and score are the same as in regular shuffleboard.

Bounce Ball

Equipment: A wastepaper basket or box, and one or more small rubber balls or old tennis balls.

Game: From a distance of from 10 to 15 feet, bounce the ball on the floor so that it will land in the box or basket.

Scoring: Five trials; 10 points for each ball in the box or basket. Double the score if all are in.

Plumb Ball

Equipment: One golf ball or sponge rubber ball suspended from the ceiling or open doorway to within 3 inches of floor.

Golf ball can be suspended by screw eye and string. Ten 5-inch pieces of broom handle or toy tenpins set up as indicated. Pin setting is facilitated if a diagram is marked on heavy cardboard or presswood. The ball is suspended to hang directly in front of the head pin.

Game: Draw the ball back and release—DO NOT THROW!

Scoring: Give 10 points for each pin knocked down on first trial. Double score if all are knocked down. Second trial if necessary to knock down remaining pins. Pins knocked down on rebound are not counted.

Spot

Equipment: Board about 18 inches square as per diagram and a rubber sink stopper, suction type. The center circle of the diagram should be at least one inch larger in diameter than the rubber stopper. Paint the circles with watercolors or oils.

Game: Lay the board flat on the floor or table, and from a distance of 6 to 10 feet, toss the rubber stopper so that it will land smooth side down on the board.

Scoring: Five trials. The score is determined by the edge of the stopper that is farthest from the center of the board.

Hole in One—Or Tossem and Catchem

Equipment: A 20-inch stick about the size of a broom handle or smaller. Attach a small tin cup or tin can with two small screws to the side of the stick and about ¾ inch from the end. From this same end suspend a sponge rubber ball on a 24-inch string. The string is threaded through the ball with a heavy needle and a small button or washer is tied to the end so that it can't be pulled back through the ball, or the ball and string may be attached to an ordinary drinking cup.

Game: Swing the ball away from you and up. Slide the tin cup under the ball when it is in the air, and gravity will help you get the ball in the cup.

Scoring: Five trials; 10 points for each catch. Double the score if all are caught.

Bull Board—Or Ferdinand

Equipment: Board 20 inches square, laid off in 4-inch squares each way and numbered as per diagram. The board may be of presswood or ¼-inch three-ply. Five small rubber heels or 5 wooden disks about 1¼ inches in diameter and ½ inch thick. To keep disks from sliding, glue coarse sandpaper to each side.

Game: Place the board on floor or table, and from a distance of 8 to 12 feet, toss the disks so that they land on the board.

Scoring: Total for all disks completely within a square. Those touching lines do not count.

Ring Toss

Equipment: Board 18 by 30 inches, ½ or ¾ inch thick, with each section painted a different color; five 6-inch rope quoits (see instructions in first section for construction of quoits). Rest the board against the wall or on an easel.

Game: From a distance of 8 to 15 feet, toss the rings on the pegs.

Scoring: As indicated.

Variation: Fasten from 8 to 12 clothespins around the top of a wastepaper basket or a card box. Toss five rubber jar rings so that they land over the pins. Allow 10 points for each pin rung. Double score if all throws are successful.

Hoop Ball

Equipment: One wire barrel hoop, five small rubber balls or five balls varying in size from a large playground ball to a golf ball.

Game: From a distance of from 8 to 12 feet, roll the balls one at a time so that they will land and stay within the hoop which is lying flat on the floor or ground.

Scoring: Give 10 points for each ball within the loop. Double the score if they are all in.

Variation: In place of the wire hoop, use an old automobile tire and a volleyball or basketball and play as above; or bounce the ball on the ground and make it land in the tire.

Hoop ball

Funnel ball

Dart target

10	20	10
	30	
	40	
	50	
	100	
10		10

Lulu-belle

Do-Do

	25	
10	5	10
20	5 DO-DO 5	20
10	5	10
	25	

Cro-bowl
or
Croquet bowling

10	25	20
	25	35
75	100	50

Funnel Ball

Equipment: One small rubber ball, a five- or ten-cent funnel, and a smooth wall.

Game: From a distance of 10 feet or more, throw the ball with the right hand so that it will hit the floor and the wall, and then catch it on the rebound from the wall in the funnel which is held in the left hand. The harder you throw the ball, the easier it is to catch.

Scoring: Four trials, 25 points for each catch. Double the score if all are caught.

Lulu-Belle

Equipment: Construct from ¼-inch three-ply or any substantial, thin piece of wood a figure as per diagram. Use your own idea as to size. Paint the features with watercolor or enamel. Suspend on a 20- to 24-inch cord a wooden curtain ring. (A rubber teething or jar ring may be used.)

Game: Swing the ring away from you and up, trying to hook it over Lulu-Belle's nose.

Scoring: Four trials; 25 points for each catch. Double score if all are successful.

Dart Target

Equipment: One board 18 to 24 inches square of soft wood or composition board glued to ¼-inch three-ply, and five feathered darts. The circles are painted on the board with watercolor or enamel.

Game: From a distance of 8 to 15 feet, toss the feathered darts, using either the underhand or the overhand method so as to make the highest possible score. The board should be placed in an upright position in front of a backing that will prevent marring of walls or damage to the darts. Several thicknesses of paperboard box will answer the purpose.

Scoring: As indicated.

Warning: Carelessly handled darts are dangerous. It will be wise to rope off a throwing space and allow no one but the thrower within this space.

Do-Do

Equipment: One board 18 to 24 inches square, ½ to ⅞ inch thick, with six penny nails or curtain hooks at points indicated in the diagram; five rubber jar rings or homemade quoits.

Game: From a distance of 6 to 10 feet, toss the rings one at a time to make them land over the hooks or nails.

Scoring: As indicated. When Do-Do is rung, player loses entire score and has to start anew. In a progressive game party, deduct 50 points from total of all games if Do-Do is rung.

Variations: Set up pop or catsup bottles in any desired diagram not to exceed two inches apart, and toss the jar rings. Give each bottle a value or allow 10 points for each "neck" rung.

Cro-Bowl—Or Croquet Bowling

Equipment: A board 20 inches square with walls 1½ inches high on three sides. The front is bevelled to provide an inclined entrance for the balls. Make eight holes large enough for a croquet ball to rest in. This can be done with an expansive bit. Provide five croquet balls.

Game: From a distance of 12 to 15 feet, roll the balls and have them land in the holes.

Scoring: As indicated.

Ring the Chair Leg

Equipment: One kitchen or folding chair, and five rubber rings constructed from bath hose. The rings should measure 4, 5, 6, 7, and 8 inches in diameter.

Game: Invert the chair and toss the rings from a distance of 8 to 12 feet one at a time so that they land around one of the chair legs.

Scoring: Give 100, 75, 50, 25, and 10 points, respectively, from the smallest to the largest ring.

Straight as an Arrow

Equipment: One small pan and five toothpicks or matches for each player. The penny-box safety matches are suitable.

Ring the chair leg

100 75 50 25 10

Straight as an arrow

Snap shot

Peanut jackstraws

Bell ringer

Gem pan polo

Game: Set the pan on a bench, and by holding the matches in the following manner, try to drop them into the pan. (In each case the match is held in the hand.)

First one dropped from the chin.

Second one dropped from the mouth.

Third one dropped from the nose.

Fourth one dropped from the right eye.

Fifth one dropped from the left eye.

Scoring: Ten points for each match in the pan. Double the score if all remain in the pan.

Snap Shot

Equipment: One 8- by 24-inch cardboard drawn as per diagram, and five small disks the size of a checker. These may be cut from a broom handle and should be ¼-inch thick. Croquinole disks will do.

Game: Place one disk on each corner of the rectangle and the other on the X. Shoot this disk as you would a croquinole disk and try to make it land in the rectangle without displacing the disks on the corners.

Scoring: Five trials; 10 points for each successful trial, and double if all are in.

Peanut Jack Straw

Equipment: Drinking glass of the size used in serving iced tea, and enough peanuts in shells to fill the glass.

Game: Each player in turn inverts the glass of peanuts on the tabletop and slowly lifts it leaving the peanuts in a compact heap. By using the fingers, he removes as many peanuts as is possible without moving any of those in the heap. He is through when a peanut moves.

Scoring: Give 10 points for each peanut successfully removed.

Bell Ringer

Equipment: A small bell suspended in a wire hoop 10 or 12 inches in diameter, and a five-cent rubber ball or old tennis ball.

Game: Suspend the hoop from an open doorway or ceiling to within 4 or 5 feet of the floor. From a distance of 8 to 15 feet, toss the ball through the hoop without ringing the bell.

Scoring: Five trials; 10 points for each time the ball goes through the hoop and 20 points if it goes through without ringing the bell.

Gem Pan Polo

Equipment: One 6-compartment muffin or gem pan (this can be painted), and five wooden cubes 1 inch square.

Game: At a distance of from 6 to 10 feet, try to toss the cubes into the compartments of the muffin pan.

Scoring: Ten points for each cube remaining in the pan. Double the score if all are in at the end, or number each side of cubes with the following numbers, one number to a side: 0, 5, 10, 15, 20, 25. Score is total of sides up.

Can Ball

Equipment: Five 1-pound coffee cans fastened on ¼-inch plywood board 20 to 24 inches square; five small beanbags about 3 inches square or five small rubber balls.

Game: Set the board on an easel or lean it against the wall, and from a distance of 10 to 15 feet, toss the beanbags or balls into the can.

Scoring: Total of score as indicated.

Bean Shooter

Equipment: Soda straw, five penny-boxes of safety matches, and small pan.

Game: From a distance of about four feet from pan, which is set on the top of a table, each player tries to blow his matches into the pan by placing them one at a time in the end of the soda straw and blowing.

Scoring: Ten points for each match in the pan, and double the score if all are in.

Can ball

Bean shooter

Ring its neck

Bottle ten pins

Over the top

Clothespin drop

Ring Its Neck

Equipment: Catsup or pop bottle, brass or wooden curtain ring suspended on a 2-foot small stick, with 20 inches of string.

Game: Try to get the ring over the neck of the bottle, which is on the floor. The stick is held at the opposite end from where string is fastened.

Scoring: Give 100 points if done in 15 seconds or less; 75 points if done in 15 to 30 seconds; 50 points if done in 30 to 45 seconds; 25 points if done in 45 to 60 seconds.

Bottle Tenpins

Equipment: Ten pop, catsup, or similar bottles, set in tenpin fashion, and large rubber ball.

Game: Roll the ball from a distance of 12 to 20 feet to try to knock the bottles over.

Scoring: Allow 10 points for each pin knocked over. Double the score if all are knocked over on first trial. Each player has second trial to knock over pins left in first trial.

Over the Top

Equipment: One 6-compartment gem pan or egg carton with dividers, golf ball or small rubber ball, one piece of three-ply or presswood about 8 inches wide and the length of the gem pan or egg carton.

Game: Set the gem pan or egg carton flat on the floor or a table and place the board so that it forms an incline up to one edge. Roll the ball from a distance of 8 to 12 feet so that it will go up the incline and land in a compartment of the pan.

Scoring: Five trials, 10 points for each successful one, and double the score if all are in. Or a value may be listed on each compartment.

Clothespin Drop

Equipment: One quart milk bottle, five clothespins, kitchen chair.

Game: Player kneels on the chair, resting right forearm on back of chair, and endeavors to drop clothespins one at a time into milk bottle, which is on the floor back of the chair.

Scoring: Ten points for each pin dropped in the bottle. Double the score if all are in.

9

Outdoor Activities and Sports

. . . . Many older adults have had a lifelong love for the out-of-doors. In pleasant weather, most people appreciate very much the opportunity to get outside. The best program planning will take this into account, especially for spring, summer, and fall.

There are many usable places outdoors: (1) the yard, if there is such, where the club meets; (2) someone's back, front, or side yard; (3) town or city parks, public places with stretches of space; (4) farms; (5) state and national parks; (6) "the woods," wherever that is; (7) camps, either for day camping or longer-term camping.

SOME OUTDOOR ACTIVITY IDEAS

1. Painting, sketching.
2. Music outdoors—concerts; visiting a band shell.
3. Nature walks in parks, on farms, in the woods, near camp.
4. Going to museums.
5. Visiting gardens for "live flower show."

6. In the fall or spring, "color tour" in cars.
7. "Block party," perhaps right in the street, which has been roped off by permission of the police.
8. Camera walk, taking pictures. (Later arrange a special time to show the pictures.)
9. "Nutting," gathering persimmons, etc.
10. "Crazy critters" hike. Look in nature for things, forms that look like persons or animals, "nature's freaks." (Might be combined with a camera walk, taking pictures of the things discovered.)
11. Bird walk, nature walk. Remember that some older adults are real specialists, and could contribute. Study wildlife, then have slides and talks.
12. A day in the country—visit to a farm.
13. Visiting sporting events (may be of the most interest to men). Going to baseball, football games, community events together. "Older adult rooting section."
14. Older adult field day (with some catchy title). Have sporting and athletic events as appropriate.
15. Old timers' picnic (more detailed suggestions for picnics further in this chapter).
16. Cookout—beans, clams, barbecue, steak fry, hamburgers/hot dogs.
17. Splash party, either for older adults themselves or in connection with the sponsoring organization, especially if a synagogue or church.
18. Trips to such places as: the airport; sporting events; band concerts; drive-in movies; the planetarium; the beach; historical spots; parks (local, state, national); zoos; shrines; other places of special interest to members.
19. Treasure hunt on a farm or in a park or other open space. The treasure is hidden and clues written out, one leading to another. People may go on the hunt in twos or in small groups. Don't make the walking too extensive. Clues might include a little knowledge of nature. "Go to such-and-such a location. If the tree there is a red oak, walk ten paces

toward the high school building. If it is a weeping willow, go fifteen paces toward Pleasant Street." The treasure might be enough refreshments for all, to be shared by the finders.

20. The backyard party (see the section on day camping for ideas).

21. Nature crafts and activities: bird feeders . . . bird houses . . . making blueprints or spatter prints of leaves, grasses, etc. . . . nature scrapbooks . . . bird watchers' scrapbooks . . . birds' nests identification . . . weather forecasting . . . star study . . . archeological explorations (Indian mounds, etc.) . . . rock and mineral collections and study . . . gardening . . . nature trails . . . tree identification . . . wild flower identification . . . animal track identification.

OUTDOOR PICNIC

(There **are** indoor picnics too, you know!)

Where? Anywhere with enough space and a pleasant atmosphere—on a farm, in a yard, at the park, near the trailer park, at some historical spot, the airport, a roadside park.

Who plans it? The special picnic committee, which may have several subcommittees—on program, food, transportation, arrangements at the grounds, equipment, publicity. Several older adult clubs might cooperate.

How do you get there? By cars, bus, chartered bus, arranged by transportation committee if it is a big enough job.

What do you do besides eat? Lots of things:

1. **General ideas:** fashion show . . . concert of the 1890's . . . "singing school" . . . storytelling . . . mock trial . . . marionette, puppet show . . . circus . . . "track meet," with real or funny events . . . music of fifty years ago . . . community singing . . . fortune-telling . . . "side shows" . . . white elephant sale . . . liar's contest . . . spelling bee.

2. **Hog Calling Contest** (as suggested by Clark Fredrickson of the National Recreation and Park Association)

   Rules for judging:

Volume, carrying capacity	30%
Enticement, appeal (sincerity, honesty)	20%
Variety (not monotonous)	20%
Originality (can tell from neighbor's)	10%
Clarity, musical quality	10%
Facial expression of caller	10%

   For "hog" might be substituted "chicken" or "husband."

3. **Guessing ideas:** Number of seeds in bottle, beans in jar, kisses in plastic bag, peanuts in container, apples in basket, amount of water in can, etc.

4. **There might be awards for:** the oldest . . . the youngest . . . the smallest foot . . . the longest name . . . the birthday nearest today . . . the person with the most buttons . . . the most grandchildren . . . the longest since their wedding . . . the biggest foot . . . the shortest name . . . the one who rode in an automobile the earliest . . . an award to each left-handed person.

5. **Equipment ideas:** plenty of tables, folding chairs, table games, even ping-pong . . . croquet equipment . . . badminton, softball, lawn bowls . . . clock golf, putting equipment . . . horseshoes and pegs . . . tossing games—metal washers, beanbags, etc. . . . beach balls . . . balloons for batting around and for balloon games . . . any of the equipment games listed in Chapter 8.

6. **Games for Picnics:** Select from group games, active games, and equipment games (Chapters 5, 7, and 8).

7. In closing, get everybody together for a community sing, and perhaps a worship service, if a religious group.

CAMPING WITH OLDER ADULTS

Generally this kind of activity falls into two categories: day camping, in which people go out only during the day, being at the "camping spot" from about nine or ten in the morning to four in the afternoon, and weekend or week-long camping in a settled camp.

Day Camping

Many older adult groups have picked this idea up from their younger forebears in the camping field, for young children have been doing it for decades. Day camping eliminates the need to have sleeping facilities, and reduces food preparation to a minimum.

If the people are not to be brought to the day camp site, it is important that it be close to public transportation, of course. If the camping is to be done in a park where tables and benches are available, care needs to be taken that proper reservations have been made well in advance.

Day camping can be done on a one-day basis or for several days in succession. It has the value of getting the people into the out-of-doors and giving them a change of scene and opportunities to visit a place of beauty and to develop skills and appreciations.

The leadership staff, of course, should be familiar with the interests, capabilities, and limitations of older adults, although everybody on the staff may not be previously skilled in working with this particular age. Older adults are usually very tolerant and appreciative.

Older adults may be involved in planning the day camp, for it is better to plan **with** than to plan **for**. The program can be quite varied. Whatever the people enjoy and want to do, they can do. If there are to be several sessions, they might like to work toward increasing their knowledge and skill, whether it be in crafts, shuffleboard playing, sketching and painting, or learning to play musical instruments, or more about the Bible or other great books.

Minimum Equipment Needed for Day Camping

1. Tables, benches, chairs.
2. Adequate supply of pure drinking water.
3. Easily accessible toilet facilities.
4. Reasonable supply of shade.
5. It is advisable to have a first-aid kit, possibly a folding cot.
6. Especially provision for making coffee, possibly for cooking total meal out of doors. It is helpful to know if some are on special diet.
7. Art and craft supplies, paints, athletic equipment as the program indicates.
8. Things for men to do. They can do most of the above if they will. Often they are neglected in activities. If some man would rather be "helpful" than do craftwork, this may be his way of showing cooperation.
9. Some might bring quilts, blankets, sleeping bags to lie on for a midday siesta.
10. Movable chairs are helpful in case the group wants to assemble for singing, etc., then disperse for activities.
11. Nature craft materials may bring a very interesting dimension. From the basic camping spot nature walks can be worked out, if you are in that kind of situation.
12. If the day camp should go to the farm of some person, it might be interesting to help with the chores. Usually equipment will be there, but some might be brought along.

Settled Camping

Older adult camps and conferences are becoming more and more popular. The conferences are often held when college is out of session, leaving available the cooking, sleeping, and eating facilities, with everything needed available. In the college or institutional setting, much activity can be outdoors, particularly sports, singing, folk dancing, and even drama, crafts, sometimes nature study. Some older adult groups like to have several delegates go to such conferences each year, even paying part of their way, and urging them to bring back good ideas.

However, out-and-out camping in camps is also growing in popularity, sometimes on a weekend basis, sometimes week-long. A good source of information is the booklet, "Summer is Ageless," available from the National Recreation and Park Association, 1700 Pennsylvania Ave., N.W., Washington, D.C. 20006.

Basics of Older Adult Camping

1. There should be an interested director who knows older adults, and who can take time to plan for the camp with them.
2. The staff, ideally, knows older adults and has been camping before, hopefully many times.
3. The camping site should have reasonably level ground and comfortable sleeping quarters, be equipped to serve good food, with distances not too great between the places the group uses.

Cabins should be smoothly floored. Beds—single, no doubles or bunks—should have comfortable but not necessarily luxurious mattresses. Space should be provided for a small table and chair beside each bed (glasses, even teeth need to be placed on a table for safekeeping overnight; a chair is more secure than the side of the bed for sitting to put on hose and shoes).

Also older people need more space than younger, as many are used to living alone and find group housing a new and sometimes disturbing experience.

There will be some married couples to plan for. When possible, a couple should be housed together. In some cases couples could not attend camp otherwise, as one person needs to care for the other. Bath and toilet facilities should be in the cabins or accessible by covered walkway.

Paths should be smooth, well-marked, and lighted.

First-aid equipment should be available in every major unit of the camp location and clearly identified. In most cases a nurse should be in the camp at all times. A nearby doctor should be on call. The kitchen staff should be apprised of specific diet requirements for individuals with diabetes, gastric problems, or other conditions. The medical history of each older camper, required at time of registration, should include medication requirements and other data to protect both the camper and the nurse who cares for him.

4. At first it may take a great deal of "doing" in arranging, publicity, registrations, etc., to get an older adult camp organized. For this reason, it is valuable to have contact with others in your area who have done older adult camping.

5. It is valuable to have a "council" meeting daily to talk over problems.

6. A rest period for one to one and a half hours after lunch is invaluable. Younger staff members may appreciate it too.

7. Activities may be as varied as those suggested in the section on day camping, and more. Camps are in nature spots, and it would be unfortunate not to take full advantage of it in nature walks, nature study, nature crafts, nature psalms, swimming, outdoor worship, particularly in the early morning or at vesper time. Also, campfires.

8. There may be a tendency to want to stay up too late, as with all people in interesting situations. The director may have to be firm. Older adults are often lonely, and hate to turn off the fellowship for mere sleep.

An older woman, in her eighties, was keeping her cabin awake with chatter at 2 A.M. "Why don't you shut up?" one asked pointedly. "Because," she rejoined, "I haven't said everything yet!"

9. It is often more convenient to charter a bus to go to camp, but a fleet of cars might be the answer.

10. The National Recreation and Park Association (address given earlier in this chapter) has several publications on older adults. They could help you with your camping needs as could members of the American Camping Association. In programming, use creative imagination. Be the first in your area to try something that makes sense!

The list of Sources at the end of this book carries titles for more thorough interpretation of camping needs than space allows here.

SPORTS FOR OLDER ADULTS

They say, in relation to pushing hand lawn mowers, that when a man's pushing sixty, that's enough! But a man in that age bracket once reminded, "The heart is a muscle, and needs regular exercise."

Older adults can play most sports except, perhaps, the body contact sports. However, those leading them should realize that the pace should be slower. Men may be out to prove that they are still physically vigorous, but simply are not realistic about their "condition." One man, proving that he could do as many push-ups as when a young man, did them, then flopped over with a heart attack. But sports in moderation add interest to any club program.

Softball and badminton are good ones. Volleyball also does not have to be strenuous to be fun. Swimming and wading are good activities for older adults when good lifeguarding is done. Beach balls add interest at the pool or at the beach.

Improvised golf games, involving putting, may be enjoyed, such as miniature golf. Older men, particularly, may enjoy getting together to go fishing, or hunting. Part of the program of any club might be to encourage members to get together in this way.

Shuffleboard, bocci ball, and lawn bowls are older adult favorites. Some play tennis. Goal-shooting with basketballs can be enjoyed. Horseshoes give a fair amount of exercise without being too strenuous for most.

Watching athletic events can be encouraged freely, and parties of men may enjoy going to see baseball, basketball, football, softball, hockey, and soccer games. It is in sports that a club can show its particular interest in the interests of men.

10

Crafts and Hobbies

. . . . Crafts make it possible for older adults to share their interests and skills with many others who need opportunities to learn new ways of expressing themselves. "Each one can teach one" (a phrase coined by octogenarian Frank Laubach in connection with literacy) and thus be useful.

To make something that has intrinsic value as well as beauty is a stimulating experience. Guidance is needed if many older adults are to have such experiences, but in most communities, it is available if you will take a bit of time to look.

If there is time and interest, assistance is available in many communities for programs of sculpturing and serious painting, including art appreciation and interpretation.

WHERE TO FIND LEADERS FOR A CRAFTS PROGRAM

1. Arts and crafts shops. They know who buys their materials.

2. Art departments in schools and colleges, including woodworking and manual training.

3. Leaders in youth organizations—Scouts, Campfire Girls, 4-H, Extension Service, camps, churches, etc.—usually know crafts people.

4. Known hobbyists who are skilled at arts and crafts.

5. Older adults themselves. Many have contacts, and some are themselves skilled in arts and crafts.

CRAFTS FOR RETIREMENT

This is the title of a very fine basic book edited by Mary Lyon for the American Craftsmen's Council, 29 W. 53rd Street, New York, N. Y. 10019, at $2.95, well worth getting for any group doing a serious craft program for older adults. It covers these ten projects from the craftsman's standpoint: hooked rugs . . . enameling . . . weaving . . . block printing . . . silk screen printing . . . hand press printing . . . jewelry and metal work . . . pottery . . . woodworking . . . needlework.

It also includes extensive lists of sources, further instructions, additional literature, and spells out costs and materials needed for both a home workshop and a center workshop.

OTHER CRAFTS (Prices given may change.)

1. **Chip carving,** done with sharp knife, razor blade. Beginner finds satisfaction; expert enjoys also. Used for wooden boxes, picture frames. *Chip Carving*, by Harris W. Moore, is published by Charles A. Bennett Co., Inc., Peoria, Ill. 61603, $1.15. Also *Modernistic Chip Carving*, by Vic Mankin, Bruce Publishing Co., Milwaukee, Wis., $1.25.

2. **Soap carving** can be a quickie project. While often done by children, it can be enjoyed by adults. *Soap Sculpture Manual* is free from the National Soap Sculpture Committee, 160 Fifth Ave., New York, N. Y. 10010.

3. **Copper tooling** and leather tooling. Many craft companies have kits. Cleveland Crafts Co., 4705 Euclid Ave., Cleveland, Ohio 44103, has an instructive booklet for 10 cents.

4. **Crepe Paper Crafts.** There is an infinite variety of craft work possible with crepe paper—flowers, table decorations, toys,

woven articles. Dennison Mfg. Co., Framingham, Mass. is a world specialist. Among the many publications of this company that you can send for is "Handcraft with Dennison Crepe Paper," 25 cents.

5. **Fly Tying.** Fishermen will like this. There is an interesting little book, *How to Tie Flies*, by E. C. Gregg, published by Ronald Press Co., New York, at $3.50.

6. **Gimp Braiding.** Fingers are the only tools needed. Very popular in camps for all ages. Most craft shops supply materials, many would have instructions. *101 Uses for Craftstrip*, by Cy Vaughn, is from Cleveland Crafts Co. (address above), at 50 cents (bracelets, tie clasps, belts, bar pins, barrettes, earrings).

7. **Leather.** Easy for the beginner; challenging to the expert! You can start with simpler projects, graduate to harder ones. *General Leathercraft*, by Raymond Cherry, published by McKnight and McKnight, Bloomington, Ill., at $1.80, gives many ideas.

8. From **The Handcrafters, Waupun, Wis.** come these very easy interesting craft projects:

HOBBY KIT. You turn the crank, watch the miracle tubing come out the bottom, then make rugs, potholders, hot pads, purses, slippers.

WEAVE A BASKET of reed, for flower-pot holders, centerpieces, candy dishes, chicken-in-the-basket, planters. Sold singly and in dozens.

PAINT A WOODEN PLATE. Instructions included.

WOODEN CROSS, especially for chip carving.

WAX CANDLE KITS, candle holder projects, honeycomb candles.

PEACOCK RULER CRAFT, to be painted, chip-carved.

MOSAIC TILE TRAYS, an attractive project.

PEACOCK 12-INCH LOOM, weaves wool, cotton, linen, silk, burlap ravelings for towels, purses, belts, handbags, scarves, table runners.

DIAMOND ART ENGRAVING tool for cutting clean, clear lines on glass, plastics, vitreous surfaces, metals. Engraving point is a diamond.

9. **Photo-Tinting.** Photography itself is a good hobby; so is tinting. *Photo Oil Painting For Fun or Profit*, by Lucille Robertson Marshall, 167 N. Ninth St., Brooklyn, N. Y., 11211. $2.50.

10. **Button Collecting.** In Ohio there is the Buckeye State Button Society, which publishes a bulletin at $1. Ethel B. Cassidy, Editor, 503 Herrick Ave., Wellington, Ohio.

HOBBY IDEAS*

Collector's Club

This would not be another group since you probably don't wish to be out every night in the week. If you belong to a "Golden Age" or similar group, this might be a sideline which would take just a few extra minutes each time you meet.

Each member selects one or two collections in which he is interested, preferably ones that do not take money. Then a list is handed out with each name followed by the things they have chosen. All members are requested to be on the lookout for these things and to bring them to the exchange held at each meeting of your group. Don't make it an even exchange, for the pleasure of finding something for another's collection is equal

---

* By J. Neal Griffith, a hobby leader of Indiana, Pa.

to your pleasure of having and adding from them for your collection. This can be a wide variety but a few suggestions will help you see the possibilities: animal pictures . . . poetry . . . recipes . . . tea bags . . . buttons . . . postmarks . . . postcards . . . history relics . . . milk bottle caps . . . pencils . . . match covers . . . jokes . . . stamps . . . tea bag labels . . . rifle shells.

Stamp Collecting—A New Departure

In past years the main purpose of the stamp collector was to get all the stamps of the world, or of one or more countries. The hobby has grown so that many think it is impossible to have a good collection and have therefore missed a lot of pleasure. A later development is topical collecting. This means settling on one or two subjects and collecting all the stamps one can find that have something to do with that subject. Some of the more popular Topical Collections are: religion, flowers, birds, animals, trains, bridges, sports, music, Lincoln, Boy and Girl Scouts, Christmas, kings, and queens. There are scores of others, and yours will probably follow something you have been interested in for a long time. With the thousands of stamps issued each year you will find that you will be interested in specializing in topical stamp collecting.

Recall

—Some of those things which gave you pleasure in the past. Was there a hobby or craft that you haven't used for years, something like refinishing furniture, making bird houses, piecing quilts, crocheting, braiding rugs, or gardening?

RECALL—Some of the friends of the past with whom you have lost contact. Write to some old friends and tell them about yourself and you'll probably get an interesting reply.

RECALL—Some book that you remembered so well that it has always given you a warm memory. It would be worth reading again and there are more libraries than ever before. You'll still find things in the Bible or in Shakespeare that you never saw before.

RECALL—The foods and drinks of the past and surprise folks with some homemade horseradish or root beer.

THE BEST FUN IS SHARED FUN.

Try Something New

Search will convince you that there is no law or maxim which says that nothing new should be tried after retirement. Older people deny themselves uncounted hours of happiness by hesitating to start something they haven't tried.

Did you wish to be a writer? Choose a subject for a day and sit down to recall with your pen or typewriter an event or memory. At least your children and grandchildren will prize it, but don't forget to send a copy to your historical society and library. Write as well as you can, of course, and perhaps you will even submit to a magazine. Such topics might be: My First Remembered Christmas; Armistice Day 1918; When the First Auto Went Through Town; The First Radio Program; Mother's Kitchen; Covered Bridges; Parties of Long Ago, etc.

Did you dream of being an artist? Well now you have the time that always seemed to be lacking. Get a few inexpensive art supplies and try your hand at sketching and painting things around you. There are good books of instruction in the stores, and there are groups nearby in which folks your age are trying their pencils and brushes. Perhaps you'll discover a talent you didn't know you had.

Do you feel a little helpless? Look around you, and you may find someone a little older or more helpless than yourself. Make a point of calling on them regularly to bring a magazine article that will interest them or a bowl of soup or glass of jelly you made yourself, to read to them if their eyes are dim, to play them an old hymn or familiar song sometimes if you have musical ability, to share your memories, to pass on a flower from your garden. If they live by themselves make a habit of calling every evening before bedtime to see that everything is all right.

If there are young folks around don't forget that all babysitters are not teen-agers. This can be a great service and sometimes a financial asset.

While you are still able, write down as much about your family tree and the members of the family, dates of births, weddings, and deaths, stories about family members, etc., as you can remember. This will become a valued asset to the folks who will come after you. Remember, many of these things you are the only one living who remembers; these will be lost if you don't put them down. Perhaps if you can't do the writing yourself you could dictate to someone else with skill at a typewriter but less memory and imagination than you.

How about your autobiography? Until you start to write, you won't realize that a lot of interesting things have happened in your lifetime. Remember that they don't have to be great things that made headlines even in the next town. Include family sayings, customs, and superstitions.

Additional Hobby Ideas (suggested by older adults themselves)

1. Artificial flowers. Also things from nature, as wreaths from seed pods, cones.
2. Home weaving of rugs.
3. Collecting and finishing odd growths from logs.
4. Rock collection, with ultraviolet light.
5. Painting, doll collecting.
6. Candle making.
7. Decorating glass, metal, wood, plastic, cloth, rubber, leather, china, crockery, and pottery; enameling jewelry.
8. Weaving mats, etc.
9. Woodworking.
10. Raising prize vegetables and flowers, hydroponics, growing ferns.
11. Raising turkey-necked frizzly and blue chickens.
12. Making rag dolls for children.
13. Nature exhibits, tree and flower specimens.
14. Playing various games, including cards.

15. The many collecting hobbies—salt shakers, buttons, ceramic animals, postcards, match covers, etc.
16. Photography, for both men and women.

Do have a **hobby show** to stimulate others in their hobbies. Many times this can be done with other older adult groups, or with age groups in community, church, or synagogue.

At a club meeting, have a "hobby lobby" occasionally. On a thumbnail-sketch basis, let someone "lobby" (Washington style) for his hobby. Some hobbies are so extensive that they should be seen in the home setting. Encourage the member to have "open house" so that others may see. Or have several "open houses" of hobbies in homes scheduled for the same evening, helping people to get from one to the other.

Drama
and Art

. . . . Going to see a good play or movie may be a most stimulating activity for an older adult group, especially if they can have refreshments and discussion afterward. Play-reading of cuttings from plays is also good. It is likely, however, that most of the "acting" will have to be short of the kind of finished performance we expect in a good play.

Scenes from group life or local and national political life; charades; embarrassing moments are all means of self-expression available to all who are willing to participate. These skits can be done at meetings or for programs, banquets, and the like. Much of the material in this section is slanted to this level.

If, however, there is a desire to do plays in the group, some suggestions are given here. The public library might help furnish collections of plays. We list some play publishers. Note that most will not send plays on approval, although some have special plans for special situations.

A play, talent night, or skit evening can provide things for all to do—costuming, scenery, lighting, script typing, advertising, and the many other tasks that must be handled for a good performance.

While it is possible to produce plays with older adults, they may much prefer doing these things:

1. Reading plays aloud, with the roles assigned, sitting around, if the group is small.
2. "Walking rehearsals," or "script in hand" plays. In this form, some advanced rehearsing has been done, and properties may be around the setting, but the actors do not have to memorize their lines. This form is a little more realistic.
3. Reading cuttings from plays. This will involve a scene, or several scenes. The parts are assigned as above.

QUALITIES OF A GOOD PLAY—FOR OLDER ADULTS OR ANY GROUP

A good play:

1. Has subject matter worthy of the actors' time.
2. Has a plot and setting related to the audience's interests.
3. Has development that gains and holds interest.
4. Has characters that seem real—real people, real life, human suffering.
5. Has action that is honest, speeches that are realistic for each character.
6. Is within the interest range and abilities of the staging group.

Now that scenery used in plays is often symbolic or suggestive, elaborate sets are unnecessary. Unless a group hired its help, it probably would not have enough energy to produce an elaborate play.

Plays "in the round," with the audience completely encircling the players, preferably on raised platforms, offer possibility. However, in many groups with a small audience, the raising of audience is not necessary.

PLAY PUBLISHERS

Catalogs of plays can be obtained free from these publishers. If specific needs are indicated to them, their consultation services furnish plays according to description. Some publishers will not send plays on approval or accept returns.

Walter H. Baker Co., 100 Summer St., Boston, Mass. 02110.

T. S. Denison & Co., Minneapolis, Minn. 55415.

Eldridge Publishing Co., Franklin, Ohio, and Denver, Colo.

Samuel French, Inc., 25 W. 45th St., New York, N. Y. 10036.

Northwestern Press, 315 Fifth Ave., S., Minneapolis, Minn. 55415.

Row, Peterson & Co., 1911 Ridge Ave., Evanston, Ill.

WRITING THEIR OWN

In addition to improvising plays and sketches as suggested, some older adults may be interested in writing and giving a play, perhaps having to do with the history of the church or synagogue or the life of an individual. (A "This Is Your Life" script would be fine!) The group might work up an idea and ask an individual or a couple to put the parts down on paper. They could work and rework the lines until they sound natural, convincing, and concise.

A good play starts in the middle (or at the beginning) of a situation having dramatic possibilities, carries this to a climax, and then works toward a satisfying resolution. Some material to be dramatized might not be play material, but simply dramatic sketches.

WHERE TO FIND IDEAS FOR SKITS AND STUNTS

Public Figures, Present and Past

Kings, queens, and leaders in general . . . George Washington . . . Napoleon-Josephine . . . Hiawatha . . . Martha Washington . . . Betsy Ross . . . Sir Walter Raleigh . . . Minnehaha . . . Queen Elizabeth . . . Robin Hood and his Merry Men . . . Romeo and Juliet . . . Hamlet . . . Shylock . . . Lady Macbeth . . .

Julius Caesar . . . movie actors, and radio and television personalities.

Poetry

There is much poetry which could be acted out for the enjoyment of skit audiences—Ogden Nash's tomfoolery . . . limericks . . . fairy stories . . . mythology . . . Cinderella . . . Alice in Wonderland . . . Rip Van Winkle . . . Jack Horner . . . the Cow That Jumped Over the Moon . . . Mother Hubbard . . . Little Boy Blue. (These stories may be modernized.)

Scenes From Daily Life

1. A man shops for his wife.
2. The small-town telephone operator does her daily work.
3. The home economist gives household hints (over radio or TV). Someone tries to follow her.
4. The Great Detective solves a case.
5. The "columnist" reports over radio or TV.
6. A man misses his bus.
7. Bus driver tries to get people to move back (and finally leaves the bus).

8. The bravery and daring of the firemen (fire engine of chairs, rescue from burning building, etc.).

9. The college student, working his way through school, sells books (door-to-door) using his printed instruction book.

10. Scene in a New York Automat.

11. A hayseed visits New York (or a city slicker visits the country).

12. Beauty parlor scene.

13. The women's club meets (one group used the letters of government "alphabet" agencies to conduct the entire business).

14. The auction sale (the fun depends on what is offered for sale).

15. The barnyard (there could be a story involving animals, with people coming forward to be the animals, or with the entire group responding with characteristic noises of animals, or acting as barnyard creatures telling what they think of people).

16. The costume shop (having various people demonstrate or model costumes for doubtful customer).

17. Style show (men or women).

18. Beauty contest (men or women).

19. The bargain counter.

20. The photography studio.

21. The crowd at the circus.

22. The first shave.

23. Scenes in an office.

24. Acting out advertising slogans (or "How 'Blank' Product Happened to Choose Its Present Slogan").

25. Preparing for that first date.

26. An aircraft welder accidentally gets rocketed to the moon.

One-Word Skits

Try giving a group just one word to start their mental processes. They are then to make up a skit around the word in twenty to forty minutes, and present it. (In some cases, two words might

be necessary.) Suggested words: ocean . . . wreck . . . mortgage
. . . blast-off . . . gallows . . . six-gun . . . cliff . . . murder . . .
north wind . . . empty bed . . . blood spot . . . flying saucer . . .
scream! . . . holdup . . . backstage mystery . . . $10,000 . . .
green eyes . . . detective badge.

Pump Primers (Ideas for Informal Drama)

1. Embarrassing situation.
2. The person is caught in his own trap.
3. Burlesque of kings and queens.
4. Dressed in clothes of opposite sex (style show).
5. Build it from scratch (forest scene or office scene). Get volunteers for scenery and for characters. Make up the skit as you go.
6. Takeoff on Western movies.
7. The great detective or international spy.
8. Woman driver.
9. Acting out folk stories.
10. Getting the children to bed.
11. A television show.

The Legend of Instant Postum*

As the narrator reads, costumed actors act out the script. If a
large group is available, with blankets, use all the characters
indicated. You can condense greatly, acting out only those characters
who seem the most important, and doubling up for characters.
Action is indicated by numbers (see at the end of the
"Legend"). Change the names of products if it improves things.

NARRATOR:

> On the shores of *Coca-Cola*
> Dwelt the *Colgates* in their wigwams (1)
> *Old Ipana* was their Chieftain, (2)
> *Pebeco,* their grizzled prophet (3)
> And the warriors, young and eager. (4)

---

* Contributed by **Harry Edgren**, Purdue University, Lafayette, Indiana.

In the lodge of the old chieftain
With *Nabisco,* "more than mother" (5)
And *Victrola,* old and feeble, (6)
Lived the warmest of the maidens,
Ovaltine, old Colgate's daughter (7)
Ovaltine, the *Sunkist Chiclet.*

All the young men sought her favor (8)
Left their troubles at her wigwam;
Brought her *Thermos* skins for raiment (9)
Also *Cuticura* ointment.
And sweet *Ovaltine* smiled on them, (10)
Smiled on *Vaseline* and *Pyrex,* (11)
Smiled on *Listerine* and *Jello* (12)
Smiled, but left them unrequited
For her love she gave to no one.

Then from *Kelvinator* Mountains
From the far heights of *Del Monte*
Came the young chief, *Instant Postum,* (13)
Mightiest hunter of the forest.

Fair he was in strength and beauty, (14)
He it was who trapped the *Kodak* (15)
He who shot the great *Sears Roebuck,* (16)
Shot him with an old *Pierce Arrow.*
Eversharp, his trusty hatchet, (17)
Every *Arrowhead* a *Hotpoint.*

On him gazed the *Colgate* maidens
Murine poured her glowing glances (18)
Bold *Fels Naptha* sought to win him, (19)
Pequot brought him cakes and honey. (20)

But for *Ovaltine* yearned *Postum* (21)
No *Pyrene* could quench the ardor (22)
That she kindled in his bosom.

Through the fields of ripe *Wheatena* (23)
Through the *Shredded Wheat* they wandered
To the *White Rock* by the river, (24)
By the rippling *Pluto Water.* (25)

There beneath the *Beechnut* shadows (26)
From the bough she picked the *Grapenuts*, (27)
There they saw the sun descending.

Naught cared *Postum* for the night winds
Blowing through the *Holeproof* forests,
Ovaltine was there beside him.

To his bosom quick he drew her, (28)
Whispered words of love a-burning,
Told her how he caught the *Clorox*, (29)
Told her how he'd slain *Bull Durham*,
Told her how he'd trapped the *Realsilk*,
Boasted of his father's teepee
With its sides so *Interwoven*
With its wings of soft *Socony*.

All the warmth of love she gave him,
All her *Hadacol* affection, (30)
Gave her heart to *Instant Postum*; (31)
There he wooed her; there he won her.

Passed the years in quick succession, (32)
Small *Post Toasties* came to bless them, (33)
Little *Wrigley*, *Spearmint*, *Dentyne*,
Seven-up and *Pepsi-Cola*,
Duz and *Anacin*, *Scott Tissue*,
These and other little *Toasties*
Filled the wigwam with their laughter. (34)

Thus we end our lyric legend,
Of the love of Indian maiden,
If you too like *Instant Postum*,
Ask by name at *Super Market*.

Suggested Action:

1. If possible, have an improvised wigwam or two.

2, 3. The old chief and prophet come out and walk up and down.

4. Likewise the young warriors, who may do a little dance.

5. Nabisco is the squaw, dressed as such.

6. Victrola is her feeble mother, creeping around.

7. Ovaltine (either a lush-looking gal or a male made up as such).

8, 9. Several of the young (of No. 4) come and bring presents indicated in No. 9.

10, 11, 12. Ovaltine smiles on them all, but looks off into distance for her unknown lover.

13. Instant Postum makes quite a show.

14. He flexes his muscles.

15. Acts out trapping an animal.

16. Acts out shooting animal.

17. Raises aloft either real or imaginary tomahawk.

18, 19, 20. Three maidens do as script says.

21. Ovaltine looks on (as 18-20 take place) and yearns openly.

22. He yearns right back.

23. Several of the cast could represent a field of Wheatena, kneeling and waving arms in the breeze.

24, 25. River scene. White Rock and River could be indicated by signs large enough for audience to read readily. (A shoe polish dauber makes quick signs.)

26, 27. She picks something from a tree. (Tree could be human, with sign.)

28. He draws her to him.

29. Broadly pantomimes his exploits.

30. She over-acts, giving him her affection.

31. If you want to, have her give him a Valentine-like heart.

32. Several people wearing signs indicating "Year" or "The Years" pass by quickly.

33, 34. If there are enough people, let them take the roles of the kiddies.

NOTE: The more ingenuity in making such a stunt as this fit the local situation, the better it will "click." Products may be substituted, of course. The narrator should read slowly enough that action can actually take place in an unhurried manner.

The Seven Ages of Man

This has wonderful possibilities for "acting out." Shakespeare had something when he put these words into the mouth of the melancholy Jacques. Seven different actors could do the parts, or one could make quick changes, doing all. A narrator reading while others act is what we had in mind as the typical way to do this as a stunt.

"All the world's a stage,
And all the men and women merely players:
They have their exits and their entrances;
And one man in his time plays many parts,
His acts being seven ages.

1. At first the infant,
   Mewling and puking in the nurse's arms.
2. Then the whining school-boy, with his satchel
   And shining morning face, creeping like snail
   Unwillingly to school.
3. And then the lover,
   Sighing like a furnace, with a woeful ballad
   Made to his mistress' eyebrow.
4. Then a soldier,
   Full of strange oaths, and bearded like the pard,
   Jealous in honour, sudden and quick in quarrel,
   Seeking the bubble reputation
   Even in the cannon's mouth.
5. And then the justice,
   In fair round belly with good capon lined,
   With eyes severe and beard of formal cut,
   Full of wise saws and modern instances;
   And so he plays his part.
6. The sixth age shifts
   Into the lean and slipper'd pantaloon,
   With spectacles on nose and pouch on side,
   His youthful hose, well saved, a world too wide
   For his shrunk shank; and his big manly voice,
   Turning again toward childish treble, pipes
   And whistles in his sound.
7. Last scene of all,
   That ends this strange eventful history,
   Is second childishness and mere oblivion,
   Sans teeth, sans eyes, sans taste, sans everything."

A Dark and Stormy Night

This dark selection has been discovered in several forms. We suggest you use it with four people reading the parts in the fashion of a musical round. **Each character is dressed in elaborate, desperate, black, flowing garments.** Actors deliver lines with exaggerated Shakespearean effect, paying no attention at all to the others who are on the stage with him or her.

At the point indicated ** below, each new character enters. This version was shared with us by Tom Washington of the University of Texas. **Each character reads skit through once completely, then leaves.**

> It was a dark and stormy night
> Just outside the gates of Paris.
> I had my rusty, trusty pistol,
> I aimed. I fired. My opponent fell
> Dead into the arms of his second!**
>
> Feeling very tired, I went to a cafe,
> A tall, dark gentleman sat at the counter.
>
> I just killed a man, said I.
> Killed a man? said he.
> Killed a man, said I.
> What was his name? said he.
> What was his name? said I.
> Yes, what was his name? said he.
> His name was Zanzibar, said I.
> How do you spell it? said he.
> How do you spell it? said I.
> Yes, how do you spell it? said he.
>
> Z-A-N, Zan; Z-I, zi; B-A-R, Zanzibar, said I.
> Z-A-N, Zan; Z-I, zi; B-A-R, Zanzibar? said he.
> Yes, Z-A-N, Zan; Z-I, zi; B-A-R, Zanzibar, said I.
> Man, you have killed my brother, said he,
> We shall have to meet!

Pilgrims Land on Steamboat Rock

NARRATOR: It was a long way to _____ (name of community) for the pilgrims. They had the Atlantic, the Great Lakes, and the _____ (local river) and the _____ (local river) rivers to cross. Finally one looked from the lookout and said _____

JOHN STEWART: Look out the lookout! Land ahead. We will call it _____ (insert name of local landmark).

PRISCILLA WELLS: Land! What a sight. All the way over, the only thing I could keep on my stomach was my hands.

JOHN: I wouldn't say I was seasick—but I sure hated to yawn!

PRISCILLA: Hush, here comes Reverend Randall. Hello, Reverend. We're almost on land.

REV.: I knew we were almost to land because things are getting better. Better buttons in the collection plate!

JOHN: Why, here come Mert and Mary Steiner.

REV.: Hello, Mert. Say I was sorry for your wife in church this morning when she had that terrific attack of coughing, and everyone turned to look at her.

MERT: Oh, you didn't need to worry about that. She was wearing a new spring hat.

MARY: Now, is that any way to talk? We've just been married a year.

PRISCILLA: Yes, I can tell you're a married man, all right. No holes in your stockings.

MERT: Yep, one of the first things my wife taught me how to do was to mend them!

PRISCILLA: Well, Mary, I suppose we'll set up housekeeping here in _____ (community) now.

MARY: Yes. Say, Prissy, I hear you and John are going to get married.

JOHN: Yep, I want a wife. I always say that a wife is a woman who will stick by you in all the trouble you wouldn't have gotten into if you hadn't married her in the first place!

The Best Music

Divide into small groups, each of which decides on a song to present to the larger group, as a chorus, quartet, solo, etc. Have one or two judges, and the one they decide on as producing the best music is given a prize. The prize may be a package of candy that all can enjoy.

Nuts

The leader calls several persons to the center of the room, addressing one as "king," another as "queen," others as "duke," "duchess," "prince," "princess," "lord," "secretary of the interior," etc. Then the leader says: "Oh, I should have told you the name of this game before we started. This game is 'Gathering of the Nuts.' " (Game is over.)

Talent Stunt

A "talent" stunt is fun; each person presents something he did in his youth. It might be a song or someone might "speak a piece" or tell some short incident of his youth; or, failing that, he might tell just a little joke or some kindness shown him.

Pantomimes

Give each person written instructions for a stunt; no words can be spoken by the actor, and the others must guess what was done. Ideas: milking a cow and pouring milk into a can . . . breaking six eggs, separating yolks and whites, and beating the whites stiff . . . knitting . . . popping corn . . . bathing the baby . . . picking a chicken . . . receiving unexpected callers . . . starting an old-time Ford.

My Most Foolish Act

Each guest tells the most foolish thing he ever did.

Paper-Bag Puppets

Here is a stunt that will be lots of fun at a party, banquet, or special occasion. Make puppet heads out of paper bags. Draw features on the bag with poster paint, tempera, or crayon. Blow up the bag, tie with a string, and attach a stick or pencil covered with a scarf under which the hand operates the puppet.

One group at a banquet put on a brief paper-bag puppet show, after every person had made a puppet. A bag with all the necessary materials was provided for each person. Guests were grouped and required to plan and present a puppet show.

Dumb Crambo

Two sides. One group goes out while the other selects a word that can be acted out, such as "trial." The other side is called back and told the word rhymes with "mile," for instance. After conferring among themselves, they make a list of words that they think might be the one selected, and decide in what order to present them. For instance, they list "smile," "rile," "style." Everybody smiles broadly to enact "smile." Then they put on a "style" show. Next they get considerably "riled." Finally they try a court scene and the other side applauds, for it's clear they've guessed "trial." The number of guesses taken is counted, and the other side goes out to try its hand at guessing and acting out the answer.

Surprise Stunts

Announce that two of the men are now going to do some very fine sheet music. Two of the group spread a bed on the floor, lie down on it, and snore.

A hitherto unheralded vocalist is announced. He is going to sing a great aria from Handel's "The Lost Sheep." A confederate strikes some thunderous chords on the piano, does a few trills and flourishes, and pauses expectantly for the solo. The soloist then loudly goes, "Ba-a-a-a-a!"

Paying the Rent

This is a good banquet stunt. The leader or a small group could present it first. Then have everyone do it in unison. The players arrange napkins to look like hair-ribbon bows, and repeat the lines in rhythm.

Landlord (deep, growling voice. Hold napkin to upper lip for mustache): "I've come for the rent! I've come for the rent!"
Heroine (falsetto voice in distress. Hold napkin to side of head like a hair bow): "But I can't pay the rent! I can't pay the rent."
Landlord: "You must pay the rent! You must pay the rent!"
Heroine: "Oh, who will pay the rent? Oh, who will pay the rent?"
Hero (manly voice. Hold napkin to neck like bow tie): "I'll pay the rent! I'll pay the rent!"
Heroine: "My hero! My hero!"
Landlord: "Curses! Curses! Curses!"

Singing Commercials

Now that singing commercials seem to be here to stay, you might as well have some stunt fun with them, too! Here are some ideas:

1. For a banquet where the group is seated at several tables, let each table make up a singing commercial about the organization sponsoring the banquet, and give it.

2. For stunt nights, preselect a theme, and have each group do both a stunt and a singing commercial. The whole program might be centered around TV.

3. Let each of several groups take the same familiar tune, like "My Bonnie" or "Jingle Bells," and see what it can work out.

4. Seasonal singing commercials. Divide the group into several smaller ones, the groupings based on the seasons. Each person joins the group of the season in which he was born. Then they do a singing commercial on that season.

5. Historical commercials. Do a commercial appropriate for the time of Julius Caesar, Columbus, Shakespeare, the Gay Nineties, etc.

Ideas for Quartet Singing

Quartets are always fun. Follow the usual pattern or try these variations:

1. **String Quartet.** After the quartet members are in place, they pass a ball of string around each other (one member holding one end) several times until they are surrounded with several strands of the string.

2. **Brass Quartet.** The group is introduced as having easily the most brass of anyone around these parts.

3. **Religious Quartet.** This could be a truly good quartet, singing good religious music in straightforward style.

4. **Topsy-Turvey Quartet.** This stunt is performed behind a sheet, blanket, or curtain. The quartet have their shoes on their hands, socks on their arms, and feet back out of sight. They arrange the shoes so that they just show under the curtain. Then, at an appropriate time, they suddenly withdraw the shoes from under the curtain, lift them up, and expose them over the top in such a way that the singers seem to be performing upside down! If the song is appropriate, so much the better.

5. **The Disappearing Quartet.** A quartet comes out to sing, with a girl accompanist. One member hits a sour note, and the leader pushes him offstage. There are lots of noises of beating, etc., behind the scenes, and the leader returns to announce that he regrets they must continue with a trio.

The same happens, one at a time, to each member of the quartet, until the leader and pianist are left. She hits a sour note. He leads her off. Loud cries and sounds of beating are heard. This time she comes back, dusting off her hands.

Pantomiming a Record

Increasing in popularity is the idea of taking a phonograph record which is performed rather dramatically (song or story) and acting it out in pantomime for an audience, while the music plays or the story is told on the record. Often this is done by one person, but sometimes a group can work it well, too. In order to make it effective, a lot of practice is needed for smoothness and for memorizing the record perfectly.

Act Out a Joke

Select a joke like the following and have members of the group act it out. Daily papers, magazines, or personal experiences will furnish ideas. It will be fun to give a copy of a joke to each of several small groups to act out in turn for each other.

Salesman (to eight-year-old, practicing the piano just inside the door): "Sonny, is your mother at home?"

Boy (with blank look): "What do you think, Mister?"

Human Calliope

This little stunt is clever for platform and banquet. Each person has a note which he sounds as the player taps him on the head. Play tunes this way (or have each pipe extend both hands, with the organist playing a tune by touching the hands of the proper pipes).

Baloney

Clever gag. One person comes out and says, "We're trying out the acoustics in here. Will everybody please be quiet for a minute." Then he puts his hand up to his face, as if he were going to call over from one mountain peak to another, and calls out, "Baloooooooooneyy!" A confederate located in another room, in the balcony, or in some faraway place responds: "Baloooooooooooneyyyyy!" in the same tone, but softer. This is tried several times, and when the first one says, "Jim Johnson is the best-looking man here," the confederate (unseen, of course) responds in echo, "Baloooooooooneyyyyy!"

Group Acting

Good for ten people or ten thousand! Someone reads out the words, and immediately when the word is heard, the people are supposed to give their reaction: fear, grief, love, hate, jealousy, envy, terror, joy, approval, disdain, and so on. One way to do it as a game is to line the crowd up into two lines, and have judges to see which line is the better.

ENJOYING AND APPRECIATING THE ARTS

Beauty is in the eye of the beholder. True, indeed. How, then, can older men and women become acquainted with those things of loveliness that will enrich their lives and help them see more beauty in everyday sights and experiences?

Why can't the club, recreation agency, temple, or church provide opportunities for people to become more familiar with great art? The task may simply be chartering buses to a nearby museum, installing a stereo hi-fi in the group's regular meeting place, or scheduling the display of a touring art exhibit. Obviously, representatives of the older adult group should participate in determining the activity, setting up schedules, and making necessary transportation or space arrangements.

Mere viewing or listening will not suffice. Many adults in the midst of their busy work years had little opportunity to discover the meaning of great painting or music. Bring someone to your group to introduce them to what they will see and hear; then the experience will really come alive for them. If the curator of the museum is not available, a teacher of art in the local schools may do the job—or a member of the local symphony or chamber music society.

Check the possibilities in these experiences with the arts. Most of these cultural activities are found in medium-to-large towns and cities. Every community has some of them.

Visits to museums to see painting . . . sculpture . . . historical artifacts . . . folk arts—weaving, carving, modeling, etc.

Concerts: attending in a group . . . discussions with maestro or individual musicians.

Drama: attending in a group . . . reading plays aloud (entire script or cuttings) . . . acting parts of play.

Music: music appreciation lectures and discussions . . . presentations by instrumentalists . . . listening to records of folk or classical music . . . musical teas . . . folk music presentations . . . listening to opera broadcasts . . . classes in piano or other instruments.

Painting, Sculpture: classes for beginners or for more advanced adult pupils . . . exhibits of work of these classes . . . exhibits of touring art displays . . . visits to great churches and public buildings to observe both architecture and art features.

Writing: exchange or original poetry . . . poetry reading hour . . . story writing . . . drama writing.

Not every retired person is going to blossom as a Grandma Moses. However, many people have for years felt the urge to write or paint or create something beautiful for the world. The Churchills and Eisenhowers are well-known representatives of a great host of people who long to do something original, unique, worthy of others' appreciation. We have suggested here a few ways in which this urge to create beauty may be given a chance and the need to recognize and appreciate beauty may be fostered in older men and women.

Fun with Music

.... Generally older people enjoy singing as much as they do games. However, some may prefer the piano, while others will want to use records.

FOLK GAMES

If records are used, it is very good to get a machine which has a slow-fast regulator for the turntable. There are several such machines on the market, such as the Rek-o-kut, Newcomb. The Califone (with variable speed) is the lowest in cost and the lightest in weight.

The "World of Fun" records* judged suitable for older folk are indicated here. Note that some have "slowed" after them, meaning that the record may be too fast for many older people

---

* Produced by the Local Division, Board of Education of The Methodist Church, these records are available in many book and record stores, in all Cokesbury bookstores, and by mail order from Cokesbury, 1600 Queen Anne Rd., Teaneck, N. J. 07666.

to follow, but can be slowed down with a machine having a turntable with variable speed control.

Work Out in Advance

New leaders, in teaching folk games, like to work them out in advance with a small experimental group. Here mistakes can be corrected before trying them on a larger group. Of course, older people who have done folk games for years will have no difficulty in picking up and going ahead, even with new material.

It would be interesting to bring in someone from another country who can tell the background of his people's folklore. (This might also include songs and stories.)

Like other people, older adults like to dress up. A folk games party might call for everyone to dress in some special costume (either authentic or improvised).

Give Breaks

After a few folk games, give older adults a rest, either with quieter games or with a complete break.

Modifications

Do not hesitate to change or modify the step to make something useful with older adult groups. Balance steps are not always easy, as in Lili Marlene. In this and other such games, the players can be made to walk in place for the particular part of the music that calls for balancing. Older folks can lose their balance rather easily, you know.

Identify women taking the part of men with a painter's cap, chef's cap, or man's hat.

Recordings

If your group has a "World of Fun" record set (with instructions), you can select the following for use with older adults:

M102 Galway Piper (Irish) (slowed) for Waves of Tory (good)
—*Come Let Us Be Joyful (German)—Danish Schottische
(*For Texas Schottische)

---

* Best for older adults.

M103 Captain Jinks (singing game)

M104 Pop! Goes the Weasel (slowed)—Camptown Races (slowed) —Red River Valley

M105 Spanish Circle—*Chimes of Dunkirk (Belgian)

M106 Green Sleeves (English)

M108 *Gustav's Skol (good)

M109 Good Humor (slowed) (for Circassian Circle)—Christ Church Bells (slowed)

M110 Newcastle (English) for Grand Square (slowed)—Spinning Waltz (Finnish)

M111 Mulberry Bush tune—Ten Little Indians tune—Oats, Peas, Beans tune—Rig-a-jig-jig (English) (slowed)

M112 Alabama Gal—Sent My Brown Jug—Sandy Land—Turn the Glasses Over (slowed)

M113 Lili Marlene (slowed)—Ten Pretty Girls—Great Big House in New Orleans

M114 *Klapptanz—Tampet

M115 *Alfelder—Sonderburg Double Quadrille (difficult)

GRAND MARCH FIGURES

Any good march tune, as Nelly Bly
Records M103, M104, M107

There is no set pattern in grand marches. The idea is to march to pleasant music, and form interesting patterns. The leader needs to preplan so that the figures will go into each other smoothly. However, if you make a mistake, laugh it off and go on.

By using care, you can end in proper formation for the next game. This will mean planning the order of the figures.

March

As the separate lines face toward the head of the room, the men are on the left, the women on the right.

1. The two lines start simultaneously. The head man turns

---

* Best for older adults.

and marches down the side of his line, the head woman down the side of her line. The others in line follow. When they meet at the foot, the man gives the lady his arm and they march up the room.

2. UP BY TWOS, FOURS, EIGHTS. When the couples reach the head of the room, the leader motions one couple to the right, another to the left, alternating down the line. These couples march down the sides of the room, and when they get to the foot of the room, come up by fours. Then the fours go right and left, alternating, when they reach the head, going to the foot once more down the sides of the room, coming up in eights. This can be continued for sixteens, etc., if desired.

3. SERPENTINE. The lines stand still in place, holding hands. The end person in the front line starts across in front of his line, then leads between the first line and the second, the second line and the third, etc., with the end person of each line joining hands with the end person of the next line below. By weaving in and out, serpentine fashion, the entire group of players can be drawn out into one circle, led into that formation by the starting player.

4. CENTER AND BACK. Here the leader may call for the circle to walk to the center and back once or twice. He or she may say, "You liked it so well, let's do it again." He may call for folks to make some joyful noises as they get to the center, then return to places.

5. PROMENADE. The group marches around the circle, men on the inside, women on the outside, facing counterclockwise.

6. FUNNY MARCHING. During the promenade, people do fancy things like: "Limp"; "Slow motion—very slow"; "Tiptoe"; "Sing"; "Prance"; "Fly"; "Swing (or turn) your partner."

7. GRAND RIGHT AND LEFT. Each person faces his partner and gives partner right hand. Then each individual moves around the circle in the direction he is facing, weaving in and out, giving right hand then left hand to the people he meets until he comes back to his partner. Then promenade again.

A number of other figures are possible.

JINGLE BELLS

(Good any time of year)   (Everybody has bells to jingle)

Formation: Single circle, partners not needed.

Action: 1. Circle left as all sing, "Dashing through the snow in a one-horse open sleigh, O'er the fields we go . . ." Then, instead of the line, "laughing all the way," all laugh, "Ha! Ha! Ha! Ha! Ha!"

2. Reverse, circling to the right, singing to the chorus. 3. Everybody jingles his jingle bells to the words, "Jingle bells, jingle bells, jingle all the way." Then walk toward the center, "Oh, what fun it is to ride in a one-horse open sleigh." 4. In the center, jingle the bells once again: "Jingle bells, jingle bells, jingle all the way." 5. Return to place back out in the circle with walking step.

GRAB, BOYS, GRAB
Tune: Skip to My Lou

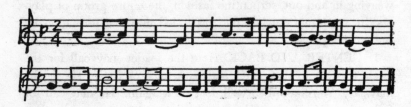

Formation: Big circle of couples, extras in the center. The song tells what to do. Everybody sings, the leader leading out.

Action (together with the song): 1. CIRCLE LEFT, Skip to my Lou (repeat two more times), Skip to my Lou, my darlin'. 2. CIRCLE RIGHT, Skip to my Lou . . . (twice more). 3. ALL TO THE CENTER, all the way in, All to the center and back again, All to the center and back again, Skip to my Lou, my darlin'. 4. TURN YOUR PARTNER, turn her 'round (repeat twice more), Skip to my Lou, my darlin'. 5. MARCH AROUND, two by two (twice more), Skip to my Lou, my darlin'. 6. LADIES TURN BACK, Skip to my Lou (repeat twice more), Skip to my Lou, my darlin'. (Here the ladies march in the opposite direction, but the men keep going on.) 7. LOST MY PARTNER, what'll I do? (twice more), Grab, men, grab. (The lines are going in opposite directions. On the first word, "Grab," the extras will try to get a partner in the opposite line. Extra women can be used as well as extra men. When you get a partner, you are ready for No. 8. If not, you have to wait until the "Ladies turn back" verse again.) 8. GET ME ANOTHER ONE, swing her (him) too (repeat twice more), Skip to my Lou, my darlin'.

Now go back to the beginning, with a circle, circling left. Repeat the whole thing as long as desired.

ACCUMULATION
(Musical game for getting partners)

Players stand in a circle, no partners. As the music plays, one or two couples march around inside the ring. When the music is stopped, each one goes to the circle to get a partner, then the music starts again. Continue until all have partners.

DAISY, DAISY
(Bicycle Built for Two)
(Singing mixer)

Formation: Double circle of couples, partners holding inside hands, facing counterclockwise.

Action: 1. Walk forward eight steps, two to a measure, swinging joined hands alone and singing. 2. Drop hands, turn about, join hands again, and swing along in the other direction for eight steps. 3. Clap own hands; slap partner's right hand with right; own hands again, slap partner's left hand with left hand. 4. Fold arms on chest, swing them gently from side to side as if rocking cradle. 5. Each man takes partner's right hand in his right, and they walk around each other. 6. Each man moves to the next woman ahead of him in the circle. REPEAT ALL WITH HER. Play as long as desired.

LOOBY LOO MIXER

The Song

(Chorus)

"Here we come, Looby Loo, here we come, Looby light,
Here we come, Looby Loo, all on a Saturday night."

(THIS PRECEDES EACH VERSE)

1. "I put my right hand in, I take my right hand out,
   I give my right hand a shake, shake, shake, and turn myself
   about."

2. Same as 1, but with left hand. (CHORUS AGAIN)

3. Same, but with both hands. (CHORUS AGAIN)

4. Same, but with right foot, then

5. left foot.

6. Whole self (step forward, step backward, shake self).

*Formation: Men to middle of room, form circle with their backs to center. Women all form a large circle around the men, facing them and holding hands. (The two circles are facing each other.)

*Action: As the song is sung, the men's circle moves clockwise, women's circle counterclockwise. When the time comes to "put the right hand in," etc., the two circles stop, leaving the men facing the women. Each goes through the action described in the song, facing one or two persons in the opposite circle, then get acquainted briefly. Here you could introduce "Fancy Handshakes" (see Chapter 4).

Repeat verses until the song is finished.

HELLO AND GOODBYE

Musical mixer   World of Fun Record M102, Galway Piper
                                 M103, Capt. Jinks
                   (Also done to "Glow Worm" or "Four Leaf Clover")

Formation: Double circle, men on inside; circle faces counterclockwise; man holds lady's left hand in his right.

Action: 1. Walk forward four steps. 2. Part in four steps. (Partners face each other; back away from each other.) 3. Each man now moves toward the lady who was at his left, as she moves toward him. 4. The new partners join right hands and walk around each other with one complete turn. They end in promenade position, ready to move forward again. REPEAT AT WILL.

Notes: It is sometimes helpful to call out a one- or two-word description of action. For this: 1. "Forward." 2. "Part." 3. "New lady." 4. "Turn." If the tune "Glow Worm" is used, the group can sing or hum it. Also "Four Leaf Clover."

---

* Variation: In single circle with leader in center, all go through the motions of 1 to 6 as they sing.

WIND THE BOBBIN (Shoemaker)

The Song

I. (a) Wind, wind, wind the bobbin, (repeat)

    (b) Pull, pull (c) tick, tack, tock.

II. Heel and toe and one, two, three. (4 times)

Formation: Double circle, man inside with lady to his right.

Action: I. (a) Partners face each other, the lady facing center, the man facing out. With fists clenched in front of chest, revolve them around each other rapidly, moving them clockwise (Measure 1). Then reverse and revolve in opposite direction (M. 2), "Wind, wind, wind the bobbin" (winding the thread). (b) Work the elbows back from one another twice as if pulling the thread (M. 3), "Pull, pull." (c) Fists clenched. Strike right fist sharply on left three times to simulate driving the pegs (M. 4), "Tick, tack, tock."

Repeat I (a), (b), and (c).

II. Partners face same direction, holding inside hands. Starting with outside foot, do a heel and toe and then three walking steps. Repeat with inside foot (Ms. 9–12).

Repeat II (Ms. 13–16). Man moves forward to next partner, and game is repeated.

SEVEN STEPS

World of Fun record M101

Here we have the Austrian version of a folk game found in various countries of Europe in differing forms, even as far north as Estonia and Finland.

Formation: In couples, with partners side by side, the lady on the right of the man, with inside hands joined. The couples arrange themselves one behind the other in circle formation. May be done in column formation with no partner changing.

Action: Seven Steps Forward (Measures 1–2). Beginning with the outside foot, the man with the left foot and the lady with the right, walk seven steps forward and pause on the eighth count.

Seven Steps Backward (Ms. 3–4). Beginning with the inside foot, walk backward seven steps and pause as before.

Three Steps Apart (M. 5). Partners release hands and, beginning with the outside foot, take three steps away from each other and pause on the fourth count of measure.

Three Steps Back Together (M. 6). Beginning with the inside foot, take three steps toward each other and pause.

Turn (Ms. 7–8). Partners turn once around in place with eight steps, holding hands as they circle.

Three Steps Apart (M. 9). Releasing their grasp, partners take three steps away from each other as in M. 5 and pause.

Three Steps Back Together (M. 10). Three steps toward a new partner and pause, the man moving forward to the next lady.

Turn (Ms. 11–12). New partners swing as before and finish in position, with inside hands joined.

The game is now repeated and continued in this manner as long as desired.

VIRGINIA REEL
Use World of Fun records M103, M104 (Sicilian Circle tune), or M107 (Brown Jug or Firemen's).

Formation: Lines of about six couples, men facing women. About six feet separate the lines. **Action:** 1. Head lady, foot gentleman walk forward and bow. Head gentleman, foot lady, forward and bow. 2. In same order, right hand swing (same people). 3. Left hand swing. 4. Both hands swing. 5. Right shoulder do-si-do. (Partners fold arms on chests, go around each other without turning around, back to back, return to places. They pass right shoulders.) 6. Head lady and gentlemen join both hands and slide (or walk) to the foot, back to place. 7. Reeling. Head couple link right arms at the head, turn around each other a time and a half, the man goes to the ladies' side and links left arms with the first lady; they go around each other. His partner is doing same action with first man in men's line. Partners meet in the center and reel a half-turn with right arms, then go on to the next person down the line. They repeat this action, left arm on the side, right arm to partner in the center, until they reach the foot. There they link arms and reel one and a half times, then return to the head. Then the man leads his line to the foot, turning to his left and going down the side of his line; the lady does the same with her line, turning to her right. The head couple meets at the foot, joins both hands, and holds them high in a two-hand arch; all the other couples go under the arch and back to place. Couple No. 2 is now in the head position. Repeat until all have been head couple.

CLAP MARLENE
Tune: Lili Marlene
World of Fun record M113 (slowed)

Formation: Circle of partners, men on the inside, women on the outside, facing counterclockwise. Hands of partners joined, man ready to start on his left foot, woman on her right.

Action:

1. Four walking steps forward, then four sliding steps.

2. Reverse direction, walk back four steps, slide four.

3. Facing partner, clap own hands, then with partner clap right hand on partner's right.

Own hands, partner's left, like above.

Clap own hands, then both hands slapped on partner's hands. Then both hands clapped together.

4. Link right arms and walk around each other in place once.

5. Repeat clapping as in No. 3, then the man moves to his left around the circle to meet the next lady, who was at his left, and bows to her. She is his new partner. Repeat all with her, from No. 1 on.

CIRCLE VIRGINIA REEL
Nelly Bly or record   World of Fun records M103, 104, 107, 112

Formation: Double circle, men with backs to center of circle, facing partners, with six feet or so separating them.

Action: (The calls in quotes)

1. **"Forward and bow."** Partners take three steps toward each other and bow/curtsy, then return to places.

2. **"Right hand swing."** Raise right hand, meet partner, join hands, circle around each other, and return to place.

3. **"Left hand swing," "both hands swing," "right arm swing," "left arm swing"** are self-explanatory, based on No. 2.

4. **"Right arm half way, left arm back."** Swing around, right arms, half way round. Shift to left arm and return to place, with a left arm swing.

5. **"Right shoulder do-si-do."** Partners advance toward each other and, passing right shoulders, pass around each other back to back. They face forward always.

6. **"Left shoulder do-si-do."** Similar to No. 5, but with left shoulders passing.

7. **"Forward and bow to the next."** Each man advances to the lady on his left, and bows to her as in No. 1 above. She becomes his new partner. Repeat all with her, then move to left again. REPEAT ALL AS LONG AS DESIRED. The special advantage of this form over the longways Virginia Reel is that everybody is in action at the same time. There are no long waits. The longways one is less active, with more time to rest.

LOTTE WALKED

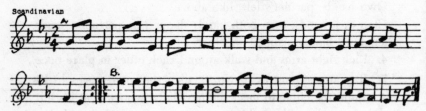

The Song:

A. Lotte walked, Lotte walked, up and down the highway,
For to see and be seen by the crowd on Sunday.
(REPEAT)

B. (Chorus) Tra-la, la-la, la-la, la . . . etc.

Formation: Double circle of partners facing counterclockwise, men on inside.

Action: There are three parts that might be called the stroll, march, and slides.

1. Partners walk around as if strolling, swinging hands along. (to ". . . on Sunday.")

2. On the repeated music, they part with a bow/curtsy and go around the circle in opposite directions, the men reversing their direction and going clockwise. (Men fold arms on chests, women hands on hips as they do this action.)

3. Chorus. Partners join both hands and do slow slides counterclockwise around the circle (four measures), then turn around each other in place (four measures). Action is repeated, but sliding clockwise this time, with turn at the end.

TEXAS SCHOTTISCHE

(This goes well with any good schottische, such as the *Danish Schottische* tune, on World of Fun record No. M102.)

Formation: Double circle of partners, men on inside, women on outside, ready to promenade. Woman raises both hands, man takes her in a cross-shoulder hold (man reaches across woman's shoulder to take her right hand in his, and across his chest to take her left hand in his).

Action: Each person takes a step diagonally forward, slightly toward center of circle, with left foot; draws right foot up to the left; steps again with left foot, pauses one count. (This takes one measure of music.) Do the same with the right foot leading, draw left to it, step right again, pause.

Next are four walking steps (left, right, left, right) to one measure of music. Then each person puts down left heel (count 1) then toe (2), and then the lady takes three quick walking steps, dropping right hand, going over to the left side (pausing on count 4). Next is right heel, toe, and three more walking steps, completing her turn and ending up at the right of the man who was behind her. She has hands raised, and the man behind takes her as his new partner.

For direction, sing (to the tune above or to "Country Gardens"): "Left, slide, left, and right, slide, right, and walk, walk, walk, walk. Heel and toe, and walk, walk, walk. Heel and toe, and walk, walk, walk."

Stealing Partners: You can take care of extras. When the "heel-toe, half-way round" part is being done, the extra woman can slip into place ahead of the regular one who plans to move back to take a partner, and the "regular" one in the circle becomes a temporary extra until next time. Likewise, the men can just stand, in front of another man in the circle, and "receive" the woman who is coming back to be somebody's partner. The man left out becomes an extra.

WAVES OF TORY
(Irish)

World of Fun record M102

Formation: Two equal lines facing each other about six feet apart, men in one, women in the other. Couples are paired into sets of two couples all up and down the line.

Action: There are four parts. Each of them is in imitation of the sea as it appeared to the folk of the little Irish island of Tory. (The tune is "Galway Piper.")

1. WAVES. Holding hands along the long lines, the two

sweep forward for three steps, raising hands high into the air on the fourth count, and retire to place. **Repeat Action.**

WHIRLPOOLS. This is a right-hand star figure. Each man No. 1 gives right hand across to girl No. 2, and girl No. 1 gives right hand to man No. 2 to form a star. A total of 8 counts are allowed for this star; shift to left-hand star and circle around in the little set 8 more counts, ending up in place in lines. **Repeat waves and star, starting with left-hand star the second time.**

2. PROMENADE (waves sweep out to sea). All face front, men offering women their right arms; the head couple leads the promenade down the women's side of the line, all couples following behind. All return to original places.

3. UNDER AND OVER (whitecaps). First couple turns to face down the line. All join inside hands. Second couple makes a single arch with joined hands; the head couple moves down the line toward the foot, going under the arch of the second couple, then makes an arch over the heads of the third couple. As the head couple approaches any couple down the line from the head, that couple becomes active and with alternating over and under positions moves from its present place to the head of the line, where the hands are dropped, each turns in place, hands are rejoined, and the couple moves to the foot and then back to its original position in line. **When any couple gets to the head or the foot it drops hands, each person turning by self, rejoining inside hands, and moves to opposite direction.**

4. CAST OFF (waves part). The head couple "casts off," and the girl leads down the outside of her line, the man down the outside of his line to the foot, each one's line following behind. As the head couple meets at the foot, it makes a double arch, and all the others go through the arch and move on toward the head.

Note: If done more than once, it needs to be noted that the composition of the stars (in No. 1 above) has changed because the first couple has stayed at the foot. It is a good idea to check the stars, beginning with the first two couples.

HERE COMES SALLY DOWN THE ALLEY
Tune: Ten Little Indians
World of Fun record M111

The Song:

1. Here comes Sally down the alley, down the alley, down the alley,

   Here come Sally down the alley, down in Alabama.
2. Hand on the shoulder and promenade (3 times), down in Alabama.
3. Swing that lady at your back (3 times), down in Alabama.

Formation: Couples stand facing in double circle, men with backs to center, both hands joined with partners to form two-hand arches.

Action:

1. Extra women start down "alley" under arches, with skip or gallop step as group sings. Just before "hand on the shoulder" line, these extra women stop beside their chosen new partner. (The women thus left without partners wait their turn next time, going to center of circle.)

2. All the rest put right hands on left shoulders of persons ahead, forming a single circle, as they sing, "Hand on the shoulder and promenade, down in Alabama."

3. "Swing that lady at your back." Man turns around to swing the woman who is behind him.

Repeat from beginning as often as desired. (If extras are men, words are changed to "Here comes Sammy.")

GOOD NIGHT, LADIES

Musical mixer—Closing

Formation: Double circle of facing partners, men on inside, women on outside.

Action: As all sing the men bow low to their partners (who curtsy) as they sing the first "Good night, ladies." Then each man moves to the left to the next woman and bows to her ("Good night ladies"). They move again left ("Good night, ladies"), and move a fourth time ("We're going to leave you now"). On the chorus, they promenade with that partner ("Merrily we roll along").

Similar action is repeated with a "Farewell, ladies" verse, and a "Sweet dreams, ladies" one may be added. The motions may be exaggerated, but should not get out of hand.

Following "Good Night, Ladies," some groups (particularly church groups) close a program on a somewhat serious note, having a fellowship circle (all stand side by side, hands crossed, holding hands with persons on either side), and singing quiet hymns and spirituals, and perhaps concluding with a prayer.

"Good Night, Ladies" may also be used in the fellowship circle. All bow low to the left, then to the right, then to center, then pause. On the "Merrily we roll along," all wave joined hands up and down, giving a sort of ocean-wave effect around the circle.

TEXAS STAR SQUARE DANCE

Music: most any lively square-dance tune

Introduction:

1. (a) "All join hands and circle south,
        Get a little moonshine in your mouth;
    (b) Come on back in the same ole track;
        Make them feet go whickety-whack.
    (c) Swing your corner, and now your own
    (d) And promenade your honey home."

Action:

(a) All eight join hands, circle left;

(b) Reverse and circle back to right;

(c) Men swing the corner (left-hand) ladies,
then swing their partners (to their right);

(d) Join hands with partners, and circle in
counterclockwise direction back to home position.

The Call:

2. (a) "Ladies to the center, now back to the bar;

(b) It's gents to the center and form a star.

(c) Right-hand star and howdy-do,

(d) Now back with the left, and how are you?

(e) Pass your own and pick up the next,

(f) Break it up as the ladies swing in and the gents swing out.

(g) Now once more, let's turn that star 'round about,
As the gents swing in and the ladies swing out.

(h) Break it up and everybody swing,

(i) Promenade home your new little thing."

Action:

(a) Ladies go in to the center a few steps, then return to places.

(b) and (c) Men form a right-hand star, holding opposite man's hand high.

(d) Reverse directions, coming back with left-hand star.

(e) Pass by the partner and men pick up the next lady (his former right-hand lady) with an elbow hook while still keeping in the star.

(f) The ladies turn into the center and form a right-hand star. The men are now on the outside, with arms still hooked through those of partners.

(g) Men once more turn in and form a left-hand star, with partners still beside them.

(h) Break up star, and everybody swings his new partner.

(i) Promenade the new partner to the men's home. (Men usually keep their original places; it is the ladies who must change.)

Chorus:

3. (a) "Allemande left with your left hand,
   (b) A right to your honey and a right and left grand.
   (c) Hurry up, boys, to the ole smokehouse,
       We'll get a little sausage in our mouths.
   (d) Meet your honey and promenade 'round,
   (e) Like a jaybird walking on frozen ground,
   (f) A-carryin' Irish 'taters, six bits a pound."

Action:

   (a) The man takes the left hand of the girl at his left in his left hand and walks once around her as she walks around him. Each returns to place, taking right hand of partner.
   (b–f) A grand right and left around the ring as woman takes partner's right hand, walks half way around him, reaching with left hand for next man's hand (his left), and continuing alternating hands in this chainlike figure until meeting partner. Each man swings his partner completely around into position on his right, then walks her back to home position, continuing in clockwise direction, using either two-handed clasp or crossed-shoulder clasp.

REPEAT CALLS NO. 2 AND 3 THREE MORE TIMES UNTIL MEN HAVE ORIGINAL PARTNERS.

Close:

4. (a) "Circle up eight and all go left,
   (b) The other way back, you're going wrong,
       Hustle around and don't take long.
   (c) Swing that gal behind you,
   (d) Now swing your own and promenade two,
   (e) Take her out like you always do."

Action:

   (a) All join hands and circle left.
   (b) Reverse direction, circling clockwise.
   (c) Men swing the corner woman
   (d) Then swing partner, and promenade with partner once around circle.
   (e) A quick swing in position and bow to partner, and that's all.

MY NAME'S JANE

(Mixer in trios)

Get into groups of three, then promenade in threes clockwise around large circle. While marching to tune of "Goodnight, Ladies," outside ones in each trio (those farthest from center of circle) sing, "My name's _____," then those nearest center respond, "My name's _____," and finally the middle ones sing, "My name's _____." All sing, "Let's go and meet the rest." Center person in each trio moves forward to join the two players ahead. All skip or march forward singing, "Merrily we roll along . . ." Then the introduction process starts again. (The leader can ask outside or inside circles to move forward instead of middle one.)

GUIDELINES TO SINGING

Think of all the many kinds of activities all ages enjoy, and you will come to music and singing again and again. For older men and women this is particularly true. Whether it's a songfest of old-time ballads or just keeping time to a quick tune on the accordion, listening to a band, or joining in a hymn sing, older folks are right in there, having a good time and asking for more. Everybody's a musician, after all, whether he's young or old, a professionally trained musician or one who can't do much more than carry a tune, and he's ready at a moment's notice to get into the gang and take part.

The most withdrawn, lonely person can be pulled out of his shell by skillful use of music. The laughter, rhythm, and sense of belonging he finds in a circle of singing, friendly people appeal to him. As he becomes more free and willing to take part, he finds his contribution appreciated by others and begins to feel a renewed sense of worth and meaning in his life. There is no experience more uniting, relaxing, or rebuilding than we find in music.

Pointers for the Song Leader

Musical activities call for some equipment, but the resourceful song leader can do a lot through using his own voice. Here are some pointers to the leader in teaching a song to an older adult group without using equipment: (1) Explain the song—the general idea, the fun in the story, etc. (2) Sing a stanza through. (3) Quote the stanza and ask the group to say it with you. (4) Ask the group to hum or sing while you sing the stanza again. (They'll be able to pick up a lot the first time.) (5) Quote the stanza again. (6) Check to see that all words are understood. (7) Try the stanza through again. (They'll probably have it by this time.)

With this easy method there will be little need for accompaniment. If the leader has a good clear voice, stands where everyone can see him easily, and shows that he's having a good time with the group; if he's not aiming for perfection in product but wants to help the people have fun in singing, the group will respond whether there's a musical instrument or not.

If there is an instrument, the accompanist and song leader should plan their procedures well in advance. See to it that the accompanist plays the written score and avoids "performing a solo while singing is going on." No more frustrating experience can be imagined than trying to sing while the pianist runs scales and shows off all sorts of dexterity. That sort of thing should be saved for a recital! The best accompaniment **supports** the singers, **guides** them, **helps them feel assured** of the melody and and rhythm. Hence, many a song leader does his own accompanying, using an accordion, an autoharp, or other instrument that unites the entire leadership in one person. He can sing, play, stop and start at will, move about in the group, use his facial movements as well as the sound of his voice and instrument to help people stay with the tempo.

Songbooks

What about songbooks? Or song sheets? First let it be said that a large-print songbook, with leaves that lie flat (thus a book with plastic rings or similar binding), is superior to almost anything else in this line. If this type is not available, every effort should be made to provide a sturdy, well-bound book with print as clear as possible. **And** a copy for each participant, by all means. People with failing eyesight, those with increasingly limited side vision, or those wearing bifocals or thick lenses can't be expected to see their neighbor's copies. Also, shaky hands can be a problem for two persons holding the same book.

Avoid song sheets like the plague! The dimly mimeographed, blurry song sheets of most of our experience, that is. If the group can't afford songbooks, the best procedure will likely be to follow the simple directions for rote learning indicated earlier. The song will go on in memory; the song sheet will become torn or lost. Some groups find a projected copy of the song useful. There are problems, however, in trying to follow the leader in semidarkness. Use this means only when others are not available.

Recordings and Group Singing

Recordings can be used to support group singing. But here again, the song leader is **the** important factor. Groups can have a wonderful time singing or whistling or humming along with the recording if they are sufficiently familiar with the song. Avoid forcing the group to sing with a recording of something they scarcely know, for they won't keep up. Tapping their fingers or patting their feet would be a better response, for everyone would be able to participate with little difficulty and no embarrassment.

"Specials" and Other Musical Activities

We have discussed group singing up to this point. Let's not forget, of course, the fun of barbershop quartets, solos, duets, and glee-club-type choruses. We like these musical features so well that we usually call them "special music," even though the same folks we see every day may be the singers. There's so much fun in trying out our voices and hearing the applause of our friends! Probably some real talent in our group just hasn't been brought out into the open recently, and here's the chance to show it off.

Other musical activities for and by older adults may include: listening to great recordings . . . group pantomime with a familiar recorded or "live" song (one with a cute-and-corny story) . . . instrumental solos or ensembles—vocal, stringed instruments, harmonicas, etc. . . . musical quizzes and contests (naming the girls' names, boys' names, geographical locations, sports, colors, etc., mentioned in titles of songs played on the piano or other instrument) . . . motion songs . . . stunt songs . . . TV and radio sing-alongs . . . learning to play an instrument—piano, organ, recorder, etc.

13

Fun at
Home

THE HOMEBOUND CAN PLAY TOO!

. . . . "Exercise is not necessary for health, but play is." Most doctors would agree with this point of view. Not only active older folks but homebound, even bedbound, men and women can enjoy laughter and singing and games and crafts. Be sure to check with doctor, nurse, or family members before you try these to avoid over-stimulating the patient or in any other way retarding his physical condition.

Provide for each homebound person a copy of your club songbook or church hymnal. When you visit, sing **with** him if he's able to join in, or **to** him if that's indicated. (Maybe a movie song guide with the little bouncing ball could be used too.) Try some motion songs so that the patient who cannot sing can participate that way.

Take a tape recording of your recent group "sing-along" and recordings of classical or light music. Check your local library for large-print songbooks so that anyone who has failing eye-sight may have help. Watch the weight of such books for it's more difficult to hold any volume when one is lying down. Avoid mimeographed song sheets. They are easily wrinkled and torn, and are often difficult to read because of inadequate inking.

Games

What games can a homebound person play? Mainly those that can be quickly completed, that require a minimum of equipment (bedclothes are perfect hiding places for jigsaw pieces!), that do not put too much demand on strength, finger dexterity, or great mental alertness. Here are some ideas:

1. **Turtle race.** Cut out freehand cardboard turtles about 9 by 12 inches overall. (Corrugated box material is the best because of weight.) Punch a small hole in the head of each and run a 12- to 15-foot string through it. With an end of each string tied to a chair across the room, you and the person in bed can wiggle your ends of the strings and "race" the turtles toward you. One rule: if the turtles get off the floor, they foul, and have to begin again. Keep them crawling. If you like, name them after two local political figures to add to the fun.

2. Imaginary "**I Spy**" or similar easy guessing games.

3. **Storytelling or singing** with hand puppets as performers.

Handwork

Keep crafts simple. Some enjoy small-loom weaving, making favors for the family dining table, cutting out pictures for the neighbor children to use at school, making wood-fiber or plastic flowers, decorating place cards with flower, bird, or flag stickers, etc.

A large lapboard, with brace to hold it at proper height, will be needed for these activities. One of the neighbors can make such a board from plywood or Masonite. A box to store materials will be needed, too. If possible, avoid crafts requiring liquid glues, or paints, heavy or extra-long scissors, and tacks or brads.

Reading Aloud

Brief periods of reading aloud will be enjoyed if the reader has a clear voice and reads with expression, and if other sounds do not conflict. "Grandfather Tales," Mark Twain's stories, the newspaper, the Bible, or other material can be chosen. Select something that can be finished in about fifteen or twenty minutes. Don't tire the listener.

Parties

Yes, parties! If the doctor approves, bring a small group (not over five or six) for an hour of chatting, yarn spinning, even singing—and, of course, refreshments. Pretty napkins, colorful refreshments (even multicolored gelatin or orange juice **looks** pretty, and doesn't disturb most food routines), and little favors make the simplest affair a party. If paper plates are used, select heavy, sturdy ones. Provide also a lapboard for the patient.

At times children's or teen-agers' groups may come to share party time with a homebound person. Keep the group small, of course.

Make a special point to celebrate each person's birthday with a cake and candles. Other special days—Valentine's Day, St. Patrick's Day, the Fourth of July, even Groundhog Day, may be cause for celebrating too.

Other Ideas

Potted flowers. The ill person can do some of the daily care, with help. Geraniums, begonias, or African violets would be lovely gifts for him to send to friends.

Try to discover something the person can do for others—telephoning for a club or campaign, sorting and filing data cards, making nut cups for a banquet, checking mailing lists, preparing mailings for a club or campaign.

Slides and movies. **You** may be getting tired of the neighbors' travel pictures, but a shut-in might well enjoy them. If the adults in the travel family aren't available, a high school boy or girl would be a grand tour commentator and projectionist.

HOME FUN FOR OLDER PEOPLE WHO AREN'T SHUT-INS

Have you tried these ideas? Test them out and add some more.

1. Telephoning—with a purpose: to sing a familiar song or hymn with a shut-in . . . to give a cheery greeting to someone who's lonely (even to share a joke) . . . to read the headlines to a blind friend (one lady has done this every day for thirteen years!) . . . to get acquainted with a new neighbor—especially if you have difficulty getting out for a visit . . . to thank someone for a kindness or congratulate a recent winner—or a person whose successes are frequently overlooked.

2. Once a week invite at least two people to share a meal with you. Nothing elaborate; there's fun just in eating together. Make a point to include a new or lonely person—especially someone you think you might not like!—occasionally. Do something nice and attractive for the table arrangements.

3. If there are children in your home (or the neighborhood) plan special things for them occasionally—a story hour, a slide show, or movie (if you don't know how to operate a projector, now's the time to learn! and the local public library has one to lend), a hand puppet show the children help create and put on, a cookie baking or whittling or knitting lesson, or even a time when they can help you with some chores.

4. Search the papers for information about museums, art shows, cooking demonstrations, and other activities that you and a friend or two can enjoy for the price of a bus fare.

5. Do you have a garden club in your area? If so, support it. If not, how about gathering some of the neighbors in your home to exchange ideas and try out skills? Start with African violets or amaryllis or maybe hydroponic gardening, so that those who live in one room can be gardeners, too. Maybe your newspaper has a round-robin seed exchange for particular plants (gourds, etc.) that you can get involved in. Seed catalogs are fun in themselves. Folks who have space outdoors might volunteer small plots for use by individuals who live in apartments.

6. Try a craft or activity you haven't attempted before: building bird houses; refinishing old furniture; painting; making pictures of dried grasses, pods, and seeds; needlepoint; tin-can crafts; making puppets; making whistles; playing the piano or other instrument; decorating lamp shades. No telling what skill you have!

7. Arrange feeders to draw birds to your yard or window. Save melon and other seeds, bread crumbs, and other food items for them. Keep a record of dates various birds appear. Write the U.S. Government Printing Office, Washington, D.C., for inexpensive booklets about proper feeders, food, and care of birds, and for instructions on how to make bird houses.

8. Don't watch TV alone **all** the time. Invite friends in, especially for the howlingly funny or particularly dramatic programs. There's more fun in enjoying a program with someone to help "chew it over" afterwards.

9. Try new recipes—and share the products.

10. Eat three regular and adequate meals daily. Even if you eat alone, set up the table or tray attractively and things will taste better.

11. Make game items for children or for your club—beanbags, alphabet cards, number cards—whatever is needed.

12. Make it a point to sing some every day—even if you have to turn off the radio to do it!

13. If you're in a three-generation household, seek ways you can add to family enjoyment: baby-sitting (not on a regular basis, for you're not an employee); serving as "chief cook and bottle

washer" for your daughter's party; taking initiative at times in a cookie baking, a family songfest, a current events discussion at the table, or a craft project.

14. Take exercises every day. If possible, get out and walk, if only for a short distance. And **walk**—don't just amble! Try a few sitting-up and stretching exercises every morning. If the TV demonstration is too strenuous, do one or two that you can manage at first, and—who knows?—you may be able to do most of the turns and twists in a few months.

15. Try to establish a routine. Avoid the purposeless wandering through the day that eats away the lives of so many people. Find something worth doing every day—if it's only giving the oven a good cleaning or sorting the thread box—and do it well.

16. Don't worry about sleeping less at night than you used to. Instead of tossing and turning, you can do some long neglected reading or see the late show and still get enough sleep to be fresh the next day. But choose something besides the latest war or spy epic!

17. As a charming eighty-year-old admonished her contemporaries, you'll have more fun if you avoid doing "old folks' dressing, old folks' cooking, and old folks' housekeeping"!

18. See also the section on service projects in Chapter 2 for home ideas.

Sources —
Books, Materials, Records

Organizations

Administration on Aging, U.S. Department of Health, Education and Welfare, Washington, D.C. Publishes *Aging* magazine.

Special Committee on Aging, U.S. Senate, Senate Office Building, Washington, D.C.

National Recreation and Park Association, 1700 Pennsylvania Ave., N.W., Washington, D.C. 20006. Publishes an annual *Guide to Books on Recreation,* including a selection of the latest books for older adults. Correspondence service. Book sales.

State commissions, councils, and committees on aging, such as Washington State's Governor's Council on Aging and Indiana's Commission on Aging. They are generally located in the state capitol; if in doubt, you could write to the Administration on Aging (see above).

Senior Citizens of America, 1424 16th St., N.W., Washington, D.C. 20036. Publishes *Modern Maturity* magazine.

CARE, 660 First Ave., New York, N. Y. 10016. Give through this organization for relief of the world's suffering.

Direct Relief Foundation, 27 E. Canon Perdido St., Santa Barbara, Calif. 93101. They get donations of drugs and medical supplies to be sent to doctors overseas. Drug firms assist, and you help pay transportation.

American Friends Service Committee, 160 N. 15th St., Philadelphia,

Pa. 19102. For decades the initiators of worthwhile service projects abroad.

Laubach Literacy, Inc., Box 131, Syracuse, N. Y. 13210. Developing literacy on a worldwide basis.

U.S. Committee for UNICEF, Box 22, Church St. Station, New York, N. Y. 10008. Performing many helpful services for the world's needy children.

Magazines and Bulletins

Aging, magazine, $1 a year, Administration on Aging publication from the Superintendent of Documents, Washington, D.C. 20402.

Modern Maturity, magazine, published by Senior Citizens of America (address given above).

Intercom, published by Foreign Policy Association, 345 E. 46th St., New York, N. Y. 10017. How to plan and use a film program.

National Council for Community Services to International Visitors, 1630 Crescent Pl., N.W., Washington, D.C. 20009. Gives assistance in helping international visitors to feel at home.

Popular Ceramics, magazine, 6061 Santa Monica Blvd., Los Angeles, Calif. 90038, $5 a year. "Clay can do wonderful things for you."

Harvest Years, "the magazine for successful retirement," 681 Market St., San Francisco, Calif. 94105, annual subscription, $4.50.

Mature Years, quarterly publication for both active and homebound older adults, Graded Press, 201 Eighth Ave., S., Nashville, Tenn. 37203.

Basic Books for Older People

Aging and Leisure, Robert Kleemeier, ed. New York: Oxford University Press, 1961.

Best Is Yet To Be, The, Paul Maves. Philadelphia: Westminster Press, 1951.

Building for Older People. New York: National Council on Aging Press, 1961. Write to the NCA Press at 104 E. 25th St., New York, N. Y. 10010 for information about this 365-page looseleaf book with vinyl cover.

Church and the Older Person, The, Robert M. Gray and David O. Moberg. Grand Rapids: Wm. B. Eerdmans Publishing Co., 1962.

Group Work With the Aged, Susan H. Kubie and Gertrude Landau. New York: International Universities Press, 1953. Out of print; see library.

Handbook of Social Gerontology, Clark Tibbitts, ed. Chicago: University of Chicago Press, 1960.

Health of Older People, Ethel Shanas. Cambridge, Mass.: Harvard University Press, 1962.

101 Ways to Enjoy Your Leisure, edited and published by the Retirement Council, Inc. New York: Harper & Row, 1964.

Recreation Activities for the Handicapped, Frederick M. Chapman. New York: Ronald Press Co., 1960. Games and other recreation activities, keyed for use with persons of particular mental or physical limitations. "The handicapped aged" is one of the categories used.

Second Forty Years, The, Edward J. Stieglitz. Philadelphia: J. B. Lippincott Co., 1946. Though not a new book, it still serves as a major contribution to the layman's study of physical aging. Out of print; see library.

Books in Social Recreation

Omnibus of Fun, The, Helen and Larry Eisenberg. New York: Association Press, 1956. This is a 640-page book with thousands of ready-to-use fun ideas for all ages, including older adults, with humor, mixers, music, dramatics, quizzes, equipment games, folk games, nature, hobbies.

Four Seasons Party and Banquet Book, The, Adelle Carlson. Nashville: Broadman Press, 1965. Contains many party and banquet ideas for all seasons of the year, attractively presented by a skillful leader.

Fun Plans for Church Recreation, Agnes Durant Pylant, ed. Nashville: Broadman Press, 1958. Contains many stimulating ideas and activities, gathered by one who herself is now an older adult.

American Citizen's Handbook, The, Joy Elmer Morgan, ed. Washington, D.C.: Senior Citizens of America (address is under "Organizations"). A tremendous collection of material for use in groups on patriotic occasions, with nearly six hundred pages of speeches and essays on citizenship by Washington, Lincoln, and others.

Summer Is Ageless, Georgene Bowen. Washington: National Recreation and Park Association (address is under "Organizations"). A 31-page rich resource for camping, special group events, and in-town activities for older adults.

Crafts

Crafts for Retirement, from American Craftsmen's Council, 29 W. 53rd St., New York, N. Y. 10019, for $2.95. A basic working manual for directors of handcraft programs for older people for hook-ing rugs, enameling, weaving, block printing, silk screen printing, hand press printing, jewelry and metalwork, pottery, woodworking, and needlework, with extensive bibliographies in each section.

Book of Arts and Crafts, The, Marguerite Ickis and Reba Esh. New York: Dover Publications, paperback ed. of book first published by Association Press in 1954. More than one thousand easy-to-do little- or no-cost crafts, including crafts for little children that might be supervised by older adults. Also woodworking, painted furniture, metal, plastics, pottery, tin, tie dying, candles, mobiles.

The Handcrafters, Waupun, Wis., publish an annual catalog of supplies. This reputable firm offers materials for cork, wood, felt, glass etching, candle craft, reedcraft, small weaving looms, metal modeling, enameling, tile craft. Directions available.

Dennison Idea Books, from Dennison Mfg. Co., Framingham, Mass. These feature things that can be made from crepe paper. Write that company for a listing of current booklets (they also can be bought in many stores).

Equipment for Fun

World-Wide Games, Delaware, Ohio 43015, manufactures and sells well-made games of quality hardwood, such as table cricket, Dutch shuffleboard, nine block puzzle, Swedish Labyrinth game, Nine Men's Morris. Annual catalog.

Recreation Research Institute, Inc., 258 Broadway, New York, N. Y. 10007, makes and sells games for older adults, such as indoor shuffleboard, quoits, croquet, electric putt-a-game, table tennis, lawn bowls, shuttlecocks.

Strayline Products Co., 336 Putnam Ave., Hamden, Conn. 06514, sells the games of Bible Lotto and Bible Quotto at $1.75 each.

Films and Plays

Superintendent of Documents, Washington, D.C. 20402:
    Films on Aging, 35 cents. A 44-page bulletin giving films, filmstrips, and suggested plays.
    Public Health Service Film Catalog, 75 cents.
    U.S. Government Films for Public Educational Use, $3, 532 pp.

National Film Board of Canada, 680 Fifth Ave., New York, N. Y. 10019. Films for rental in the United States.

Health Education Visual Aids, from The Film Library, North Carolina State Board of Health, Raleigh, N.C.

Three plays by Nora Stirling, dealing sensitively with problems of aging:

Choice to Make, A, one-act play on self-concepts in aging. Family Service Association of America, *Plays for Living,* 44 E. 23rd St., New York, N. Y. 10010.

Ever Since April, a play on retirement. American Association of Retired Persons, Dupont Circle Bldg., Washington, D.C.

Room Upstairs, The. A family adjusts to an aging person. Human Relations Aids, 104 E. 25th St., New York, N. Y. 10010. A set of copies for production (6 copies) is $4.

Other film sources: mental health sources, state universities, churches.

Music

Let's Sing. Little Falls, Minn.: Transcript Publishing Co. Cleverly enlarged words, letters one fourth of an inch high, for about fifty familiar songs and hymns popular with older adults.

357 Songs We Love to Sing. Chicago: Hall-McCreary, Publisher. A large collection with piano accompaniments.

How to Lead Group Singing. New York: Association Press, $1. Variety of suggestions on having a good program of singing for groups.

Twice 55 Brown Book (for general singing), *Twice 55 Blue Book* (men's voices), and *Twice 55 Rose Book* (women's voices). Moderately-priced songbooks from C. C. Birchard, 221 Columbus Ave., Boston, Mass.

Look Away (Negro spirituals) and *Song in the Air* (Christmas carols). Fine, inexpensive collections from Cooperative Recreation Service, Delaware, Ohio.

General Suggestions

Hydroponics. Description of soilless growing of plants from Charles C. Gilbert & Co., 830 W. Ivy St., San Diego, Calif. 92101.

Starting a Recreation Program in Institutions for the Ill or Handicapped Aged. Morton Thompson. Washington: National Recreation and Park Association (address is under "Organizations"). A helpful booklet for $1.25.

Aging in Indiana, Harry Edgren, ed., Commission on Aging, 1015 State Office Bldg., Indianapolis, Ind. 46204. Practical suggestions by Indianans for senior citizens in music, drama, out-of-doors activities, hobbies, dancing, volunteer services.

Program Aids. A fine bulletin duplicated by The Governor's Council on Aging, Box 1162, Olympia, Wash.

Giant-Sized Posters are three-foot-high travel posters from about fifty countries for decorating club and home, available from Box 526, Norristown, Pa. 19404, at $1 each, $5 for six, and minimum order of three.

On the Mend, guide to recreation in hospitals, from International Recreation Association, 345 E. 46th St., New York, N. Y. 10017, for $1.

Are You Planning on Living the Rest of Your Life? A booklet with clever questions for an individual or for a program, from the Superintendent of Documents, Washington, D.C., 20402, for 30 cents.

INVENTORY 74

INVENTORY 1983